Elton Sherwin

PRAISE FOR *THE SILICON VALLEY WAY*

---

*"A 'feel good' business book which is enjoyable to read.
It deserves a wide audience."*
—KYLE ROBINSON, PRESIDENT,
DANWIRE MANUFACTURING

---

*"A concise and clear business planning approach
that is applicable to service products as well as
hardware and software products. It works."*
—ELIN KLASEEN, SRI

"[The Silicon Valley Way] . . . *the discipline
your creativity needs to create a successful product."*
—ANNE ROYALTY, PH. D., ASSISTANT PROFESSOR,
STANFORD UNIVERSITY, DEPARTMENT OF ECONOMICS

---

*"Most business planning books are more daunting than
starting a new business.* The Silicon Valley Way
*makes it easy. Real nuts and bolts advice on how to
identify a good business idea—and what to do with it."*
—DR. MICHAEL W. DULA,
STRATEGIC PLANNING CONSULTANT

THE SILICON VALLEY WAY

The Silicon Valley Way

■ ■ ■

Discover the Secret of America's
Fastest Growing Companies

■ ■ ■

Elton B. Sherwin, Jr.

PRIMA PUBLISHING

PRIMA PUBLISHING and colophon are registered trademarks of Prima Communications, Inc.

DISCLAIMER
This publication is sold with the understanding that the author and publisher are not engaged in rendering legal, accounting, or other professional services. Your situation may differ from those described in this book. If legal, accounting, or expert assistance is required, the services of a competent professional should be sought.

The author and publisher specifically disclaim any liability, loss, or risk, personal or otherwise, which is incurred as a consequence, directly or indirectly, of the use and application of any of the contents of this book.

Interior Design: Melanie Haage

Interior Art: Betsy Grimes

Library of Congress Cataloging-in-Publication Data
Sherwin, Elton B., Jr.
The Silicon Valley way : discover the secret of America's
fastest growing companies / by Elton B. Sherwin.
p   cm.
Includes index.
ISBN 0-7615-1272-1
1. Industrial management. 2. New products—Evaluation.
3. New business enterprises—Evaluation. I. Title.
HD31.S452   1997
658.5'036—dc21   97-37282
CIP
98 99 00 01 02 HH 10 9 8 7 6 5 4 3 2 1
Printed in the United States of America

How to Order
Single copies may be ordered from Prima Publishing, P.O. Box 1260BK, Rocklin, CA 95677; telephone (916) 632-4400. Quantity discounts are also available. On your letterhead, include information concerning the intended use of the books and the number of books you wish to purchase.

Visit us online at http://www.primapublishing.com

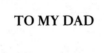

TO MY DAD

CONTENTS

ACKNOWLEDGMENTS

I would like to thank the many individuals who reviewed drafts of *The Silicon Valley Way*. I am particularly grateful to: Kyle Robinson of DanWire Manufacturing, Kay Brown of PREMIER Biosoft International, Elin Klaseen of SRI International, Jim Coughlin of StarTemps, Inc., Dr. Michael Bowles of Crosspoint Venture Partners, Anne Royalty, Ph.D., of Stanford University, and Marketta Silvera of Pilot Network Services, Inc. Dr. Michael W. Dula, Dr. John Seybold, Dr. Jack Wenstrand, Mary Lynn Robinson, Judy Mohr, Hans Wijmans, Brad Bueermann, and Barry Hegarty provided advice, enthusiasm, and moral support, which helped more than they realize.

My thanks also go to Ann Winblad, Eugene Kleiner, and John Doerr for authorizing the reprinting of excerpts from prior interviews.

I am obliged to Scott A. Ryles, Roy L. Rogers, John Montgomery, Professor William M. Cockrum, and Dale L. Fuller who endured interview sessions and are quoted in various places throughout the book.

I am deeply indebted to Anne Morris for her legal advice and to Betsy Grimes for her swing-set artwork. My thanks to Dr. Barr Taylor for helping me find my agent, Sheryl Fullerton, who steered *The Silicon Valley Way* throughout the hallways of the publishing industry.

And finally, I would like to acknowledge the enormous contribution of my wife, Katharine, who has simultaneously critiqued and encouraged this manuscript.

INTRODUCTION

Global Leadership

Smaller than Rhode Island, Silicon Valley is home to over 7,500 high-tech companies. It is America's leading exporter of manufactured goods. A prolific developer of new technologies, it leads the U.S. in patent awards. In less than 20 years, it has become the undisputed global technology leader, consuming one-third of America's high-tech venture capital and developing many of the world's most innovative products.[1]

The Valley's culture of innovation thrives on the challenge of turning new technologies into profitable companies. Once dominated by military electronics and semiconductor manufacturing, Silicon Valley has diversified. Today, its economy includes thousands of companies specializing in software, computer hardware, telecommunications, biotech, and the Internet.

The Valley's success at creating new products, new companies, and new industries has attracted investment from around the world. Daimler Benz has a research facility two blocks from Stanford University. Fujitsu has *eight* Silicon Valley locations. Merrill Lynch has moved their information technology practice from San Francisco to Palo Alto—not to save money (which is unlikely since Palo Alto office rents now rival Manhattan's), but to be closer to their high-tech customers.

Intel, Hewlett Packard, Sun, Cisco, Seagate, Adobe, Oracle, Intuit, and a myriad of lesser-known companies have thousands of openings for engineering and marketing professionals. Their collective success—their ability to innovate—has made the Valley famous. Governments attempting to replicate this success are modeling their high-tech centers on Silicon Valley. Around the globe *forty* municipalities have added "Silicon" into their moniker, including Silicon Mesa and Silicon Bayou.

Silicon Valley has become the global metaphor for innovation and leadership.

AMERICA'S HIDDEN SUCCESS STORY

The arrival of the microprocessor accelerated the pace of technology and business planning. The silicon chip created many new industries and each new industry created thousands of business opportunities. This explosion of opportunity made traditional business planning techniques obsolete and overwhelmed many organizations.

Silicon Valley executives adapted to this whirlwind of technology-driven change. At the eye of the storm, they developed techniques to evaluate these new projects quickly and effectively. Over time, they learned to ask the right questions and became adept at picking winners.

The Silicon Valley Way is a behind-the-scenes look at the American high-tech miracle. It describes a uniquely American management style—a business planning methodology—that enables fast, high-quality decisions.

SILICON VALLEY:
BIRTHPLACE OF THE MICROPROCESSOR

Why Silicon Valley happened in Santa Clara County is a topic of debate. Valley executives most frequently attribute the success of Silicon Valley to four factors:

Stanford University and the University of California. These two great universities—their business schools, their medical centers, and their schools of engineering and computer science—created the nucleus of the high-tech industry, which now attracts top technical talent from around the world.

Venture Capital. The availability of financing for high-risk projects—an art form pioneered in Northern California—enabled many small companies to obtain financing unavailable in other regions and countries.

The Concentration of High-Tech Companies. The concentration of 7,000 high-tech companies has created a self-sustaining culture of innovation. Parents and grandparents expect their children to work for unknown companies and change jobs frequently. Engineers and executives jump to small, high-risk enterprises, confident that other opportunities will be available should their current company fail.

The Weather. Surprisingly, many executives mention the weather as a major reason they keep their businesses in Silicon Valley. With 300 days of sunshine, the area has an idyllic climate for outdoor enthusiasts. Hiking, cycling, sailing, tennis, and golf are available year-round. Employees addicted to the Valley's outdoor lifestyle are often unwilling to relocate.

These factors have played a major role in shaping the Valley's success, but they are not the whole story. If the availability of capital and a well-educated, mobile workforce were sufficient to create a "Silicon Valley Clone," other states would have replicated this Northern California success. No municipality has succeeded in duplicating the Valley's prosperity, in part because the formula includes other subtle ingredients:

Workforce Diversity. Silicon Valley has one of the most diverse and best-educated workforces in the nation. Hispanic, Asian, and many other cultures blend, creating a uniquely American workforce—innovative and hardworking.[2]

Two-Income Families. In Silicon Valley, double incomes often provide financial security, enabling one spouse to leave a secure job and join a start-up. Entrepreneurs whose spouses have stable incomes are more willing to take career risks. In many countries, Japan in particular, workforce inequality restricts the mobility of both men and women, shrinking the size of the labor pool available to start-ups.

Labor Laws. American entrepreneurs are able to start new companies because, unlike their European counterparts, they can dismantle them. European entrepreneurs are reluctant to start new companies because firing employees and shutting down a failed start-up is so expensive. The laws designed to protect workers actually prevent the creation of new, well-paid, high-tech jobs.

Government and Industry Cooperation. The economic slowdown in the early 1990s caused many local Silicon Valley governments to become more business-friendly. They streamlined their building permit process and adopted more consistent building codes. San Jose, for example, cut its approval process for minor building permits from two weeks to one day. For some major commercial developments, the process was reduced from six months to one month. By 1997, San Jose had ten million square feet under construction and the Valley had created 100,000 new jobs.[3]

California's Culture. Californians value the intuition and interpersonal openness required to innovate. Often ridiculed, California's mantra of "get in touch with your feelings and share your emotions," has subtly shaped how California's engineers and financiers communicate with each other. The Valley's culture of truth-telling and personal accountability creates an environment where companies build prototypes because an engineer "feels the technology will work."

Employee Ownership and Stock Options. The granting of stock options to non-executives—engineers and marketing professionals—has enabled new companies to compete for talent with larger, more established enterprises. Stock options enable entrepreneurs to start companies quickly, exploiting new technologies and markets.

California's Public Colleges. California's state colleges and junior colleges play an important role in developing the Valley's workforce. In many European and Asian states, it is difficult for workers to change professions. In California, late-bloomers can obtain a college degree and change careers. Many countries exclude some of their brightest minds from high-tech careers because of poor grades or test scores early in life. Everyone gets a second chance in California. This increases the size, quality, and mobility of Silicon Valley's high-tech workforce.

California's Pioneer Mentality. In the 1850s, young miners moved from claim to claim searching for the "big strike," and San Francisco financiers made huge investments too risky for their East coast counterparts. A century later, this pioneer spirit continues in Silicon Valley; young engineers change companies, searching for the "big product," and investors fund start-ups too risky for their Eastern peers.

TRANSFORMING RESEARCH INTO GOLD

Valley executives have outperformed many of their more established competitors. They have mastered the complex art of transforming research technology into profitable products. Valley entrepreneurs win at the high-risk game of technology roulette, succeeding where others have lost fortunes.

This modern alchemy—turning research and technology into gold—has eluded many larger, better financed companies. Valley executives have become so adept at developing new technologies that many companies are now investing in Silicon Valley for fear of being outmaneuvered by their smaller, nimbler Valley competitors.

DISCIPLINE AT HIGH SPEEDS

In some high-tech enterprises, 50% of next year's revenue will come from products not yet shipping. Some companies, like Hewlett Packard, remain nimble, continually producing innovative products. Other companies, like IBM in the 1980s, dominate an industry and then lose their ability to develop new, winning products. Occasionally companies return from the brink of disaster, betting on a winner, as Chrysler did with the introduction of the minivan.

Silicon Valley executives are like Indy car racers. They are disciplined and fast, often appearing reckless and making observers nervous. Like great Indy racers, great entrepreneurs are rare, perhaps because disciplined analysis at high speeds is hard.

WINNING IN THE SILICON CENTURY

Between 1984 and 1994, over 250 companies left the Fortune 500. Some of these companies merged with larger companies and a few rebounded, later returning to the Fortune 500. But most of the companies, almost half of the Fortune 500, were replaced by their once-smaller competitors. These giants of American industry invested in the wrong products or the wrong markets. They failed to pick winners.

Many companies around the world continue to evaluate new ideas haphazardly. They invest poorly, sinking millions in businesses with little chance of success. They spend heavily on internal research and development, yet never develop leadership products. They have large marketing departments, yet always miss the fastest growing markets.

To win in the twenty-first century, you will need to:

- Pick the right markets
- Know your customers
- Design exceptional products
- Market your products creatively
- Distribute your products efficiently

The Silicon Valley Way poses the questions you will need to answer if you are to successfully compete in a high-tech world. In a few hours, you will get help organizing your thoughts and planning your business.

HOW TO USE THIS BOOK

The Silicon Valley Way contains a collection of forty-four techniques used by the Valley's most successful entrepreneurs and executives. Short and pragmatic, the book includes numerous mini-case studies and examples.

The Silicon Valley Way describes how Valley executives develop their business plans in a variety of situations. Some chapters are likely to prove more useful than others, depending on your situation. Here are a few suggestions on when and how to best take advantage of *The Silicon Valley Way*:

Starting a New Business. If you are starting a new business, you may find it helpful to organize your thoughts in the format of a "Business Strategy Presentation" shown on page 122. Then read the entire book, paying particular attention to the last two chapters, "Confronting the Truth" and "Raising Money," which start on pages 88 and 100 respectively.

Running a Small Business. If you already run a small business, read the book quickly and dog-ear the pages that seem most relevant to your business. Then go back to these pages and pick the three that seem most urgent. Focus on one area each week for the next three weeks. This is a bit like picking a recipe from a cookbook. Select the ones that you think will work for you.

Developing a New Product. If you are developing a new product, jump to the appendix and evaluate your plans using the *Product Development Scorecard* and the *Marketing, Sales, and Distribution Scorecard,* which start on pages 130 and 132. Then develop a *Product Concept Document* similar to the one shown on page 120. On a monthly basis, track your progress by scoring yourself against these scorecards. Consider publishing or posting your scores along with your schedule (see page 52) and your competitive feature matrix (see page 55).[4]

Investing in Another Business. If you are contemplating making a significant financial investment in someone else's business, analyze the opportunity using the techniques shown on pages 4, 20, 34, 55, 94, 107, and 130–134. These criteria are tough and may help you avoid opportunities destined for failure.

Raising Money. If your business concept is well defined, and you are looking for funding, start with *Confronting the Truth* on page 88, then read the remainder of the book, including the appendices. If your product concept or business model is poorly defined, start with chapter 1 and read the entire book, filling in the blanks as you go along.

Writing a Business Plan. If you are writing a business plan, start with *The Business Plan Outline* on page 129. Make sure you know who your target audience is, by reviewing the advice on pages 101 and 127. Consider developing a *Business Strategy Presentation* similar to the one on page 122 before you write the business plan.

USING THIS BOOK IN LARGE CORPORATIONS

The Silicon Valley Way can help corporations develop better products and make more effective investments. Techniques presented are especially useful during:

Quarterly Business Unit Reviews. *The Seven Question Executives Ask* (pages 6 to 21) is a good outline for a business review. *What are the current products? Who is buying them? How many are selling?* cover the basics frequently obscured in corporate reviews. Developing a structured format for quarterly reviews will enable you to compare one business unit's ongoing performance with results of other units. In addition, consider expanding your quarterly review package to include the techniques dealing with market planning, competitive analysis, and product scheduling shown on pages 34–40 and pages 53, 55, and 84.

Acquisitions and Major Investments. Developing a consistent format for analyzing potential new businesses and acquisitions will improve your investment decisions. Start with *The 45-Second Business Plan* on page 4 and the *Product Concept Document* on page 120. If these look promising, develop a *Business Strategy Presentation,* as outlined on page 122.

New Product Announcements. A formal review process of *all* product announcements will improve your marketing efficiency and may prevent the introduction of incomplete or ill-conceived products. A product launch review should start with *The 45-Second Business Plan* (page 4), and include a schedule (page 52), as well as the details on pricing, distribution, and marketing plans (pages 70–85).

FICTIONAL COMPANIES

The following companies and their stories are fictional. Any resemblance to real companies, their products, or employees is purely coincidental. With almost 8,000 high-tech companies in Silicon Valley, I may inadvertently have used a real company's name. If I have used your name by mistake, my sincerest apologies. I have renamed Portola Hills Software four times, as the first three fictional names were subsequently used by real start-ups.

Andy's Deli

Atherton Flower Boutique

bigvcfirm.com

Bounce Electronics

Coyote Creek Gas Station

Cupertino E-Mail

Cupertino Missile Guidance Systems

Dave's Warehouse

Enviro Displays

Heinrich's Hofbrau

Homeward Bound Flower Cart

L'Chef

Math Magicians

Palo Alto Boheme

Palo Alto Hospital

Palo Alto PC Company

Portola Hills Software

Sand Hill Venture News

Santa Clara Satellite

Silicon Deli

Silicon Valley Repertory Theater

Sunnyvale Server

THE SILICON VALLEY WAY

The Back-of-a-Napkin Analysis

Jump to the Bottom Line

■ ■ ■

What tips me off that a business will be successful is that they have a narrow focus of what they want to do, and they plan a sufficient amount of effort and money to do it. Focus is essential. . . .

—EUGENE KLEINER, VENTURE CAPITALIST,
as quoted by Rhonda Abrams in
The Successful Business Plan: Secrets & Strategies
(Oasis Press, 1991)

■ ■ ■

Central to the success of Silicon Valley is the entrepreneurial skill of evaluating new ideas quickly. Executives sketch products on napkins and analyze cash flows on business cards during lunch meetings. They evaluate and discard potential projects in rapid succession.

If you were to eavesdrop on such a lunch meeting from an adjacent table, the conversation would sound disjointed. Speakers hop from one topic to the next, interrupting each other and answering their own questions. Slowly, a pattern emerges. The speakers are asking each other the same questions over and over.

Successful Valley executives employ a methodology. Their mantra of probing questions is actually a mini-business case: "What is the product? Who is the customer? How much will it cost?"

The 45-Second Business Plan outlines the seven questions executives most frequently ask themselves and aspiring entrepreneurs. If you lunch in Woodside, Palo Alto, or Santa Clara, you are likely to hear these questions asked and answered.

The 45-Second Business Plan

■ ■ ■

**I try to avoid lengthy business plans,
since too much detail clouds simple concepts.**

—Roy L. Rogers,
Rogers Investment Corp.

■ ■ ■

Fill in the Following:
Do *not* attach additional sheets; do *not* use more space than
provided.

1. What is your product?

2. Who is the customer?

3. Who will sell it?

4. How many people will buy it?

5. How much will it cost to design and build?

6. What is the sales price?

7. When will you break even?

If you cannot summarize it in the space provided above,
your idea will be difficult to explain to others.

■ ■ ■

THE ENTHUSIASTIC NOVICE

A young engineer had a clever idea for a new product: an automotive collision avoidance system. Since his department was not responsible for automotive products, his manager asked him to present the idea to his division general manager.

The general manager asked several questions, but did not seem excited about the technology. He said he would look into the idea, but nothing ever came of it.

What went wrong? The young engineer could not answer these three simple questions:

- Is there any demand for such a product?
- How much would it cost to build?
- Who would sell it?

The young engineer understood the technology, but he had not priced the parts nor had he talked with anyone in marketing. He did not know the answers to the basic questions executives and investors ask.

Before you write a business plan, before you present to the "big cheese," answer the seven questions of The 45-Second Business Plan.

■ ■ ■

CHAPTER TWO

Seven Questions Executives Ask

■ ■ ■

At HP, as in other technical companies,
there is no shortage of ideas.
The problem is to select those likely to fill
a *real need* in the marketplace. To warrant
serious pursuit, an idea must be both practical
(the device under consideration
must work properly) and useful.

—DAVID PACKARD,
COFOUNDER OF HEWLETT PACKARD
as quoted from
The HP Way: How Bill Hewlett and I Built Our Company
(HarperCollins, 1995)

■ ■ ■

TOO MUCH PLANNING CREATES PARALYSIS

Many large organizations have cumbersome, formal processes designed to prevent projects from being initiated without approval. Bureaucratic approvals usually stifle creativity without minimizing risk. They prevent knowledge gained in one generation of product from being passed on to the next. They ensure that successful developers and product managers rarely succeed a second time. Bureaucracy typically creates products that are mediocre, expensive, and late to market.

NOT ENOUGH PLANNING CREATES CHAOS

Some divisions of large companies and many start-ups have no planning process. Managers start projects with no documented plan. Executives, engineers, and entrepreneurs all forego planning at times, and the result is usually fuzzy thinking and internal conflict.

EFFECTIVE PLANNING CREATES SUCCESS

Successful executives encourage their organizations to plan effectively. While encouraging innovation, they also try to prevent premature, ineffective action. Successful executives often guide their organizations by asking a small number of questions that focus on the critical success factors relevant to their business. Likewise, successful investors ask similar questions before investing their money.

The following seven questions expand on the basics of The 45-Second Business Plan. Each focuses on one of the seven questions most frequently asked by successful executives. The answers provide the essentials needed to develop a successful new business, product, or service.

WHAT IS YOUR PRODUCT?

DESCRIBE THE PRODUCT IN ONE SENTENCE

Focus your efforts by developing a one-sentence description of your product. It should capture the essence of your product and contain its key measurable objectives. This descriptive sentence will be the yardstick you use to determine which features are critical to your success.

Scott Cook, cofounder of Intuit, had a vision that people could balance a checkbook using PC software and do it faster than they could with a pencil. He gave the product a name that encapsulated his goal: Quicken. From this simple but astute objective—to balance a checkbook faster—Quicken overtook forty-two competitors and became the number one selling personal finance software in America.

Craft a simple-to-understand, one-sentence description of your product or service, making sure it contains a measurable objective so you will know when you have achieved your goal.

The product will

This single sentence is the core of your business plan; it will keep you focused on your target. The examples on the following page illustrate this technique.

■　■　■

ONE-SENTENCE PRODUCT PLANS

A leading edge PC. Develop a multimedia home PC for under $500.

A children's bicycle. Manufacture a colorful children's bicycle branded with Disney characters retailing for under $69.

A child safety lock. Design an unbreakable child safety lock for cabinets and drawers that installs without tools.

A combined light bulb and motion detector. Develop a light bulb which fits standard lamp fixtures that will automatically turn itself off when the room is empty.

A laser that tracks drivers' eye movements. Design an automotive early warning system that "sees" where a driver is looking and beeps when the driver's attention wanders from the road.

■　■　■

WHO IS THE CUSTOMER?

WHO WILL BUY YOUR PRODUCT?

Be specific. In a quest for a hit product, it is tempting to think of everyone as a prospective buyer. Products designed to satisfy everyone's needs have too many features and cost too much. Target everyone and you will please no one. The following list illustrates how you can better target a vague market:

Too Vague	Better
PC Owners	Users of Windows 95
TV viewers	Viewers of the home shopping channel
Homeowners	Homeowners painting their homes
Teenagers	Teenage boys, 16–18 years old

A specific target market also makes the product faster to design and easier to package. Although it may seem counter-intuitive, the *smaller* the market, the *more* you will sell.

Complete the following sentence:

The buyers of my product will be

■ ■ ■

A CONTRAST IN BLOOMS

The Homeward Bound Flower Cart

Located at the main train station, between the ticket counter and the tracks, the Homeward Bound Flower Cart's primary customers are businesspeople. Because the flowers are wrapped and ready to go, commuters can buy a bouquet in under 30 seconds.

The Atherton Flower Boutique

In contrast, the Atherton Flower Boutique caters to its wealthy residents. Located in one of America's most expensive suburbs, selection and personalized service are key to its success.

The customer, not the product, determines the type of service and packaging that will succeed. The upscale suburban flower shop delivers personalized service, a large inventory, and hand-wrapped bouquets. The railway flower shop delivers pre-wrapped flowers quickly. While both sell flowers, each meets a different set of customers' needs.

Identify your customer. This will help you determine where to sell the product, how to price it, and which features are critical to your success.

■ ■ ■

WHO WILL SELL IT?

■ ■ ■

**New companies often expend too much cash on
overdone product development efforts, and are
then unable to mount strong marketing efforts.**

—WILLIAM M. COCKRUM, PROFESSOR,
Anderson School of Management at UCLA

■ ■ ■

Who will sell your product? Frequently overlooked, the
sales channel can become your Achilles' heel. Critical because it is your source of revenue, the sales channel will
also help determine product elements such as key features, retail price, packaging, wholesale price, support
plan, and advertising strategy.

Decide who will sell your product before you build and
box it.[5] Products sold in superstores look different and may
require different features than products sold on the Web.

Spend time with your potential distributors and dealers. Interview them and ask them how many they can sell.
A sales estimate from a distributor or channel partner can
sell others on your idea and help you raise money to develop your product. Complete the following sentence:

The sellers of my product will be

■ ■ ■

CAN YOU SELL YOUR PRODUCT ON THE WEB?

A Web site with product information is quickly becoming a necessity in most industries. But this does not mean the Web will find new customers. It may, in fact, not sell your product at all. To predict whether the Web will generate new sales for a consumer product, answer the following questions:

	No	Yes
Self-explanatory? Does the name or picture alone describe the product's purpose?	☐	☐
Bought via credit card? Will most buyers use credit cards?	☐	☐
Easy to demonstrate? Is a free demo on the Web feasible?	☐	☐
Easy to install? Can most buyers install the product themselves?	☐	☐
Are catalogs available? Are similar products successfully sold on the Web or in catalogs?	☐	☐

TOTALS

Mostly No: This product should be sold by salespeople or systems integrators. ____

Mostly Yes: This product can be sold on the Web and in catalogs. ____

■ ■ ■

HOW MANY PEOPLE WILL BUY IT?

FIGURE ON 1/10% OF YOUR TARGET CUSTOMERS

Imagine having an idea, building something, and persuading 250,000 Americans to send you a check in your first year of operation.

One-tenth of one percent of America is 250,000 people. This is an aggressive goal. Don't be conned into thinking you can do 30% of the total market in year one unless you have a lot of experience and are in a unique situation, such as developing a cure for a disease or having a firm order from a large customer.

Total Market Size	
Multiply by 1/10%	$\times .001$
First Year Sales Estimate[6]	

■ ■ ■

ASPIRING MAGAZINE MAGNATES

In some industries, selling the product *before* it is built is worthwhile. Aspiring magazine publishers occasionally solicit subscribers for a yet-to-be-written magazine. They mail solicitations that look real—with a name, price, and a list of articles—to prospective subscribers. If no one responds, the magazine concept is discarded. If 2% of the people respond to a small mailing, the aspiring entrepreneur can predict that 2% will respond to a larger mailing.

SELLING LARGE CUSTOMERS

Many entrepreneurs approach their largest potential customers before they build their product. This works well for products targeted at corporate customers.

These are not surefire techniques since determining how many people will buy a product before it is built is extremely difficult. Often you just have to build the product. Everyone struggles with this issue; it gives even seasoned professionals headaches.

■ ■ ■

How Much Will It Cost?

HOW MUCH MONEY WILL YOU NEED?

Many seasoned executives can quickly estimate the costs of developing a new product or starting a new business. Through experience they develop an understanding of the key ratios in their industry. They take one or two pieces of data—the number of beds in a hospital or the size of a wafer fab (semiconductor plant)—and estimate how much cash it takes to run the business.[7]

The following example uses the size of the engineering team to estimate the annual expenses of a software company. Build a similar template for your business and it will enable you to estimate costs like a seasoned pro.

		Example
Salary of an Engineer	$_____	$100,000
Equipment, benefits, etc.	× 2	× 2
Number of engineers	× _____	× 10
Total annual cost of R&D	$_____	$2,000,000
SG&A[8] (Sales, General, and Administrative)		
Multiply by 3 the cost of R&D	× 3	× 3
Total of SG&A	$_____	$6,000,000
Operating Expenses – excluding production		
(Total of R&D plus SG&A)	$_____	$8,000,000

■ ■ ■

SILICON DELI'S
ESPRESSO MACHINE

Silicon Deli, known as "Andy's" to the locals, made the best sandwiches in the Valley. Engineers and office workers queued up midday in front of Andy's small shop. The business was profitable.

One afternoon a salesperson sold Andy an espresso machine. Andy quickly saw how profitable espresso is. "Very high gross margins," the salesperson explained.

The line in front of his store lengthened, but he sold fewer sandwiches. Revenues declined and profits disappeared.

What went wrong?

Andy ignored his labor costs. Espresso is a labor-intense business. If espresso were like salad, assembled earlier in the day, it would have been very profitable. Andy had idle capacity at 10:30 but none at 12:30. His marginal cost of labor soared to $28 per hour during lunch.[9]

How much will it cost to build your product? This is often very difficult to calculate, but it is worth the effort. If you do not know, it may be impossible to predict whether you will make any money.

■ ■ ■

How Much
Will You Charge?

■ ■ ■

**New companies, afraid of losing a sale, often
under-price their products.**

—William M. Cockrum, professor,
Anderson School of Management at UCLA

■ ■ ■

Prices come down over time. When you enter the market,
you will create more competition and prices may come
down further. If you create a great product, competitors
may have to reduce their prices even more to compete
with you.

Premium Pricing = Today's Price. If you plan to have premium components, excellent manuals, stellar technical
support, and highly paid salespeople, figure you may be
able to charge what your competitors charge today.

Normal Pricing = 70% of Today's Price. As prices de-
cline and competition heats up, plan on getting 70% of
your competitors' current price in two to three years.

Breakthrough Pricing = 50% of Today's Price. Charge
50% of your competitors' price and you may be able to
expand the size of the market.

■ ■ ■

ENVIRO DISPLAYS

Founded by two Stanford physicists, Enviro Displays has designed a new low-power computer monitor that won awards at recent trade shows.

Cost-Plus Pricing

A major PC manufacturer sees an article about Enviro's monitor in *PC Week*. Impressed with the prototype, the company asks for a bid of 10,000 units to test the market for a new line of executive PCs. Enviro takes the cost of setting up a small plant, the cost of parts and labor, and divides by 10,000. They add 50% to cover overhead and submit the bid.

Enviro Displays loses the bid to a Japanese company.

Head-in-the-Ground Pricing

Enviro failed to do their homework. They did not do the following:

- Talk with the customer about price before submitting a bid.
- Discover what competitors typically charge their large customers.

The combination of burdening early customers with 100% of your overhead and ignoring competitors' prices often results in failure, particularly for products with strong competition.

■ ■ ■

WHEN WILL YOU BREAK EVEN?

DEVELOP A P&L STATEMENT

To develop a P&L (profit and loss statement), start by fore-
casting your revenue for each of several years. Then calculate your expenses for each year. When will your revenues
exceed your expenses? Except for pharmaceuticals and
biotech, most executives want a profit in the second or
third year.[10]

A software company might look like this:

	Year 1	Year 2
Annual Sales:		
Price (Question 6)	$_____	$_____
Times Annual Volumes (Question 4)	×_____	×_____
Equals the Sales Revenue	$_____	$_____
Expenses:		
Manufacturing Expenses (Parts, Packaging, etc.)	-_____	-_____
Operating Expenses (Question 5)	-_____	-_____
Profit (or Loss)[11] (Revenues/Expenses)	$_____	$_____

■ ■ ■

THE SILICON INSIDER'S CASH FLOW PROBLEM

The Silicon Insider was the largest distributor of supplies to the semiconductor industry. Nicknamed "Dave's Warehouse" by the Valley's purchasing agents, it offered a large inventory at low prices.

Flamboyant and frequently mentioned in the press, Dave had built his business "on cash." He never borrowed money and disliked bankers. His controller urged him to set up a line of credit, but Dave knew better than to be tempted by credit.

Then the semiconductor industry had a slow year. A reporter speculated that the Silicon Insider would be hit hard by the industry downturn. The story started a rumor that Dave was in trouble. Soon all of Dave's suppliers demanded cash before delivering new merchandise.

Starved for inventory, Dave's business declined. Seven months later he declared bankruptcy.

The Silicon Insider had been profitable in three of the past five years. Had Dave paid attention to his cash flow, and had an established line of credit, he would have weathered the bad times and would be profitable today.[12]

■ ■ ■

Most failures are caused by poor husbandry of cash resource. The bottom line is: Never run out of cash.

—WILLIAM M. COCKRUM, PROFESSOR, Anderson School of Management at UCLA

■ ■ ■

Market Research

■ ■ ■

The only kind of market research
that impresses me is to see
what you've learned from
testing your product in the real world. . . .

—ANN WINBLAD, PARTNER,
HUMMER WINBLAD VENTURE PARTNERS,
AS QUOTED BY RHONDA M. ABRAMS IN
The Successful Business Plan: Secrets & Strategies
(Oasis Press, 1991)

■ ■ ■

Market research is a collection of related techniques that are beneficial when used skillfully and at the right time, but become expensive distractions when executed poorly or at the wrong time. Market research falls into several broad categories:

Demographic and Statistical Data. How many potential buyers are there for your product or service? This is the most common—and frequently the most important—part of market research. Data from government agencies, industry associations, the press, consultants, and the Web are used to build a profile of potential buyers.

Competitive Data. Who are your competitors and what are they doing? Collected from many sources, competitive data describes your competitors' products, prices, customers, marketing strategy, technical specifications, distribution channels, and financial health.

User Surveys. What do users think about current products or competitors' products? This information gathering is often done over the phone or in front of a store.

Focus Groups. Can potential buyers predict their future behavior? Groups of individuals are shown pictures or prototypes of potential products and then are questioned about their likes and dislikes.

Usability Testing. Can potential buyers figure out how to use the product? Prospective buyers are often videotaped using the product; observers then study and use the results to refine the product.

Most successful companies collect demographic and statistical data about their customers and their competitors. Many companies also do usability testing before shipping a new product. Focus groups and user surveys are less common but can be very beneficial, particularly for consumer products.

WHAT DO
THE NEIGHBORS THINK?

DO THEY OFFER TO INVEST MONEY?

I once had an idea for a 900 number, a fee-based telephone information service. It was great idea—such a great idea that I kept it secret lest a neighbor decide to steal it and start their own 900 number.[13]

Because I am not very good at keeping secrets about exciting ideas, I spilled the beans one evening to the elderly couple next door, who were unlikely to start their own 900 number. They were decidedly cool to the idea. I saw this as unfortunate, since they were in the target market for my product. It turns out that retired people do not think much of spending money on 900 numbers.

I learned three things from this experience:

1. Ask neighbors for their opinions.
2. Listen carefully to what they actually say (not to what you want to hear).
3. Recognize that neighbors sometimes give good advice.

A further survey of the target market confirmed my neighbor's response—retired people do not think much of spending money on 900-number information calls.

■ ■ ■

THE APPLE NEWTON

In the fall of 1993 Apple Computer planned one of the most dramatic product introductions in Valley history. The public relations campaign was enormously effective. The press wrote hundreds of stories and Apple received almost limitless free advertising.

Everyone knew the Apple Newton was coming. Unfortunately, like the space Shuttle Challenger, the product had one small, but fatal, technical flaw. The feature at the core of the media hype—handwriting recognition—worked poorly for many consumers.

Had Apple management shown the engineering prototype to a few of their neighbors, they could have avoided a public relations disaster. Any neighbor would have told them the handwriting recognition was not ready for the mass market. Had they taken the time to talk with their neighbors, they could have saved themselves much embarrassment.

No matter how compelling your story, take the time to personally show the product to your friends and neighbors. It's cheap, it's neighborly, and it can save you from embarrassing yourself in public.

■ ■ ■

What Does the Media Think?

VISIT A PUBLIC LIBRARY

Public libraries can help you survey a topic and see how it appears in the general media. Junior college libraries are also good resources. University research libraries may drown you in detail.

Talk with the reference librarian. Be specific. *Ask for directions.*

Start with a written list of topics and companies to research:

Competitors

Critical Technologies

Potential Customers

You should review at least one CD-based index to current publications and the most recent issues of the *Readers' Guide to Periodical Literature.* Depending on the topic, you may need from three to thirty hours to exhaust the periodicals in a typical public library. Print or photocopy anything you may wish to include in your business plan.

■　■　■

BOUNCE ELECTRONICS

After leaving the Air Force two decades earlier, Paul Yearwood worked for Cupertino Missile Guidance Systems. A dedicated employee, Paul, now 47, planned to retire there. Fate intervened.

Two years ago Paul offended a Pentagon procurement bureaucrat. The following year the Pentagon audited his department, reviewing every document Paul had ever signed. Shaken, Paul survived, but his career in military electronics was dead. With three kids to put through college, he was worried.

Paul put together his resume and began to talk with headhunters. A small boutique headhunting firm in Woodside set up an interview with Bounce Electronics, a 20-person start-up developer of satellite systems for the Internet. Satellite systems were Paul's area of expertise, but he knew little about the commercial Internet.

Paul spent the weekend at the Cupertino Public Library. He studied up on the World Wide Web and developed a vision of how to use satellite technology on the Internet.

Eight interviews later, impressed with Paul's thoughtful style, Bounce hired Paul as their Director of Electrical Design. Bounce had interviewed thirteen younger candidates. Convinced that his weekend in the library got him the job, Paul is now a major contributor to the Cupertino Public Library.

■　■　■

WHAT'S ON THE WEB?

**THE WEB HAS BECOME
A POWERFUL MARKET RESEARCH TOOL**

Some tips for doing research on the Internet:

1. **Some companies monitor Web usage.** If you work for a company, do not use their network for outside projects. If you are setting up a new business, get your own Internet account at home.[14]

2. **Many companies log all faxes, phone calls, and e-mail.** If you are working on an outside project, keep it separate from your current job.[15]

3. **If you are new to the Web,** start by researching a topic you know well and assessing the results.

4. **Use lots of bookmarks.**[16]

5. **Talk to people who do research on the Web.** If you are researching a product for a large company, corporate headquarters will have a reference library or strategy office. Call and ask for assistance.

6. **Use the fastest modem** supported by your ISP (Internet Service Provider).

7. **Copy relevant material to your hard drive.** Later, you may need to include it in a presentation or business plan.

8. **Be skeptical.** Most Web sites are selling things. They may not contain the whole truth.

■ ■ ■

MATH MAGICIANS, INC.

Professor John Zeitman watched with envy as several of his colleagues left academia and started their own companies. Zeitman knew little about business, but he was an expert in encryption and data compression, two branches of mathematics that enable electronic commerce to flow more quickly and securely.

Professor Zeitman decided to start his own company to develop mathematical algorithms for Internet commerce. Zeitman used the Web to research his potential competitors and was depressed to find dozens of companies already developing compression and encryption products. His wife suggested he meet with the CEOs of these start-ups.

The first company he approached used Russian mathematicians (many of whom were ex-KGB) and was very secretive. Paul learned little about their business.

With some trepidation, Paul approached Math Magicians, a small venture capital-backed start-up. Their CEO immediately understood the value of Paul's skills. They struck a deal in which Paul would consult with Math Magicians in return for stock options.

■ ■ ■

WHAT DO THE EXPERTS SAY?

■ ■ ■

**Consultants who develop market estimates
using data supplied from manufacturers
often overstate the market size.**

—SCOTT A. RYLES, MANAGING DIRECTOR AND HEAD
OF GLOBAL INVESTMENT BANKING,
Merrill Lynch

■ ■ ■

Interview the experts in your industry. This obligatory exercise can be frustrating if the experts say it cannot be done, or recommend you buy their services.

Don't be unnerved if an expert does not like your idea. Keep an open mind, listen carefully to his or her opinions, and then adjust your plan as necessary. You are not seeking approval. You interview the industry expert to formulate a response. For example:

"Alan Whitmore, a leading industry expert, believes _____. I [agree/disagree] because of _____. In light of this, I have adjusted the business plan to conserve cash and reflect the possibility that revenues will take longer to develop. . . ."

Money people may bet against expert opinion, but they usually do it knowingly. Do not ask for money until you know what the experts say.

■ ■ ■

HIRING A CONSULTANT

Get the Free Samples

Most consultants will give you a copy of their newsletter and a sample of their work. Some have Web sites you can browse. You may find it helpful to buy back-copies of their newsletter as well. Larger consulting firms frequently publish studies, for a fee, on specific topics. Buy the study and read it before you hire the consultant who wrote it.

Know Why You Want a Consultant

Identify your specific reason for employing a consultant. For example, do you want to:

- Audit a project?
- Fix a problem?
- Obtain technical advice?
- Subcontract a specific task?
- Put a stamp of approval on a product?

Read the Whole Contract

Pay close attention to the confidentiality and intellectual property clauses.

Check References and Personality

Ask to talk with prior customers who needed similar services. A great technician might not be the right person to present to the board. A smooth talker might not be the right person to solve a tough manufacturing glitch.

■ ■ ■

WHAT DO THE NUMBERS SAY?

■ ■ ■

Make sure there is a market.

—ROY L. ROGERS,
Rogers Investment Corp.

■ ■ ■

Finding good data that supports your business plan is often difficult, because forecasts on emerging markets are ambiguous, market segmentation is frequently unclear, and reports are often out of date.

Nevertheless, as you research a topic, collect *all* the numbers, and:

Save all the data. No matter how tangential or irrelevant it may seem, save all the revenue and market size data you can find. Copy it to your hard drive or make photocopies, but do not leave any numbers behind.

Save the source of the data. Without a source to quote, you will find it difficult to use the numbers later.

Do not worry that the numbers are contradictory. The market segmentation may be different from yours. Product planners get upset if their segmentation differs from industry experts and often want to redo the business plan. It does not matter. Live with a little ambiguity in life.

■ ■ ■

THE COYOTE CREEK GAS STATION

Hank recently inherited a small garlic farm from his uncle. Located south of Gilroy at the Coyote Creek Road interchange with the interstate, the property is adjacent to a new McDonald's. Hank decides that the location is good for a gas station and convenience store. He wonders how many customers a day he could attract.

Notebook and stopwatch in hand, Hank spends a week visiting gas stations at freeway exits. He measures how many cars leave a typical freeway exit to buy gas, how many cars buy gas at similar intersections, and how many cars buy gas at service stations next to a McDonald's. He collects the following data:

	Cars per Day	% Buying Gas	Projected Gas Station Customers
Freeway Traffic	100,000	0.1%	100
Coyote Creek Road Traffic	12,000	1%	120
McDonald's on an Interstate	2,500	10%	250

Hank is a bit unnerved by the contradictory data, but it convinces him that his critical success factor is the percentage of McDonald's customers he can entice to buy gas. He designs his gas station with easy access to the McDonald's and goes on to have a very successful business.[17]

■ ■ ■

CAN YOU PREDICT
THE FUTURE?

■ ■ ■

**They had a great product and a great technology,
but they were too far ahead of the market. . . .
It was the right product, just the wrong time.**

—JOHN MONTGOMERY, PARTNER,
General Counsel Associates, LLP

■ ■ ■

Most business strategies are predicated on a set of assumptions. Many entrepreneurs spend enormous energy convincing themselves and others that their visions are correct, and that they can predict the future.

Prudent businesspeople analyze the market forces that will affect the success of their business. They know that certain demographic trends can make or break a business. Take the example of an Internet-ready portable classroom—a portable classroom with large flat-panel display and a satellite link to the Internet:

Prospects for an Internet-Ready Portable Classroom

School-Age Population	Per Student Expenditures ($)		
	Declining	Stable	Growing
Growing	C+	B+	A
Stable	D	C	B-
Declining	F	D	C-

■ ■ ■

SANTA CLARA SATELLITE'S LOST SNEAKER

Santa Clara Satellite had developed an inexpensive-to-manufacture, unbreakable geo-positioning system. They had inserted the device with a transmitter into a kid's sneaker and it was very reliable at finding lost children.

Santa Clara Satellite analyzed the opportunity and determined that the cost of manufacture—not yet known—and the public's perception of the crime rate were the key variables determining their opportunity.

The company then developed a plan for each possible future.

Developing strategies for multiple eventualities is an extremely powerful technique. It forces you to plan for an uncertain future and also encourages you to develop strategies for higher costs and more difficult economic times. Here is how Santa Clara Satellite analyzed the lost child business:

Prospects and Strategies for a Sneaker with an Imbedded Geo-Positioning System

Crime Rate	Cost of Manufacture:	
	Under $50	Over $50
High or Increasing	**A** Invest heavily in plant and marketing	**B** Outsource manufacturing and market to wealthy
Low or Declining	**B** Test market to see whether mass market works	**D** Poor business; wait for high-profile kidnapping

■ ■ ■

The Competition

Know Your Competition

■ ■ ■

Have lunch or be lunch.

—Scott McNealy, CEO,
Sun Microsystems

■ ■ ■

Knowing your competition will help you hone your thinking, refine your financial plan, and develop a better product.

Successful Silicon Valley companies know their competition. Some do formal research, most do informal research, but all know a lot about their competitors. Engineers disassemble their competitors' products. Lawyers read their competitors' patents. And salespeople examine their competitors' Web sites.

Look beyond the product. High-tech professionals focus on their competitors' products. Engineers usually want to attack the functional deficiencies of their rivals. They try to build a better mousetrap. Often they can. Unfortunately, many who are designing a better version of their competitor's flagship product assume they should attack the flagship product. This strategy is frequently ill-conceived.

Instead, examine the bigger picture. Look for *all* the opportunities. Perhaps you should address a new market or even become a supplier to a larger player. To see all the opportunity, scrutinize the competition on every conceivable metric, examining such aspects as:

- Distribution Network
- Suppliers
- Location
- Finances

- Patent Filings
- Customer Service
- Alliance Partnerships
- Customer Base

Entering your competitor's market with a slightly better product is like opening the third ice cream shop in a small town. It is a tough way to make a living. Look instead for markets that the competition has overlooked.[18]

WHO IS YOUR COMPETITION?

■ ■ ■

**You have to assume that there is someone out there
as smart or smarter than you, someone who is
already building the product you want to build.
You need to find out who they are.**

—ROY L. ROGERS,
Rogers Investment Corp.

■ ■ ■

Who are your top five competitors *today?* List them below.

1.

2.

3.

4.

5.

Who are your toughest *potential* competitors? Who could
enter the market or increase their investment and really
hurt you? List them below, including at least one foreign
company:

1.

2.

3.

4.

5.

■ ■ ■

ANDY'S COMPETITION:
PART I—WHO ARE THEY?

Andy has sold his espresso machine (see page 17) and business has returned to normal, but it is not as profitable. Andy can no longer find minimum-wage workers willing to work short shifts. He has increased wages and has been forced to schedule longer shifts. His labor costs have eroded his profits.

Andy understands his local competitors, most notably:

- **McDonald's**
- **La Boulangerie**
- **Heinrich's Hofbrau**

While these competitors are formidable, their restaurants are also six to eight times larger than Andy's and are therefore unable to locate in prime downtown real estate.

Andy's near-death experience with the espresso machine has made him more cautious. He decides to check out his future competitors. He is particularly worried about two:

- **Starbucks**
- **New York Bagels**

Andy takes the train to San Francisco and . . . (continued on page 41).

■ ■ ■

WHAT ARE THEY DOING?

WHAT ARE THEY THINKING?

How much do you know about your competitors? It is often helpful to you—and impressive to potential investors—to organize your thoughts in a table, for example:

Competitor's Name:	
Largest Customers:	
Key Business Partners:	
Financial Health:	
Market Share:	
Skills They Hire:	
Key Products:	
Product Price:	
Product's Key Features:	
Who Sells the Product:	

You may already have much of the above information and simply need to organize it in a table. Short answers are often better than long answers; for example, "strong finances" or "hiring many salespeople" is sufficient.

■ ■ ■

ANDY'S COMPETITION: PART II—WHAT ARE THEY DOING?

Andy arrives in San Francisco and quickly becomes very worried. Starbucks, New York Bagels, and even McDonald's have figured out how to survive in much less real estate and are moving into prime downtown locations. Worse, they are able to attract customers six to ten hours a day, spreading their fixed costs.

Andy sees his two key competitive advantages—lower rent and lower labor costs—disappearing. Worried, he returns to Silicon Valley and makes several changes:

- Installs thermos coffee canisters so he can brew coffee during slow times and sell it all day.

- Installs a cookie oven and bakes "Andy's Chocolate Chip Cookies" in the mornings and afternoons.

- Posts a sign: "Call in orders of 5 or more sandwiches by 10 A.M. and pick up before noon."

These changes help Andy generate more revenue during his slow times. This also spreads his fixed costs—primarily rent—over a larger revenue base, increasing his gross margins. So without hiring new staff, Andy increases his revenue by $3,000 a week.

■ ■ ■

WHAT IS THEIR
VALUE PROPOSITION?

WHY DO PEOPLE BUY
YOUR COMPETITOR'S PRODUCT?

Why do some shoppers buy name brands over generics? Why is one PC more popular than another? Try this exercise with your major competitors. Check each box that describes why consumers buy your competitor's product. Then allocate the retail price of their product in the blanks next to the check marks.

This is surprisingly difficult. Take the example of a $2.19 jar of Grey Poupon mustard. Which boxes would you check, and how would you allocate the $2.19 among them?

Knowing the consumers' alternatives often helps. In the Grey Poupon example, the store brand's basic yellow mustard costs $.79 and the store brand's Dijon mustard costs $1.39. Does this influence how you define Grey Poupon's value?

Defining your competitors' value proposition will help you define what is important in your product (answers on page 135).

☐ Save Time	$____	☐ Lower Risk	$____
☐ Save Money	$____	☐ Maintain Status	$____
☐ Make Money	$____	☐ Enjoy Life	$____
		☐ Improve Comfort	$____
		☐ Survive (a necessity)	$____
		☐ _____ Other	$____

■ ■ ■

CUPERTINO E-MAIL

A small software start-up, Cupertino E-Mail, was developing a new e-mail package for an already crowded market. Unfortunately, marketing and engineering could not agree on a product specification. The product manager insisted that the product needed certain features. Engineering was equally adamant that the product manager was wrong.

As the bickering continued, development floundered. Finally, marketing backed down and ceded the design of the product to engineering. The product manager ripped up his 65-page specification document and produced a 2-page marketing requirements document which emphasized saving time.

Marketing developed benchmarks to measure the time spent:

• On unwanted e-mail

• Opening and answering of e-mail

Motivated to improve their benchmark scores, engineering rapidly developed a series of patentable innovations and a very successful product.

Cupertino E-Mail succeeded because they picked the right value proposition and then rapidly improved the product until their benchmark scores beat those of their competitors.

■ ■ ■

WHAT ARE THEIR SECRETS?

DOING BUSINESS LEAVES TRACES

Early signs of competitive activities are found in sources
such as:

The Sunday "Want Ads" in the local newspaper. Read
the want ads in your competitors' local newspapers.
Some newspapers post their help-wanted ads on the
Web and some utilize fax services.[19]

Job Postings on the Web. Many companies post job openings
on their Web sites. These can be a gold mine of information.

Lexis-Nexis. Access to the Lexis-Nexis online database is
expensive and is therefore often overlooked. Because
Lexis-Nexis is comprehensive and can yield almost
complete histories of press coverage and litigation, you
may find the service worth the expense.

Trade Shows. Visit your competitors' booths at trade
shows. Closely watch their demonstrations.

E-Mail Search Services. Several search services will automatically scan the news each morning and e-mail or fax
you the results.[20]

Marketing Materials. Advertisements, fact sheets, user
manuals, product packaging, and Web sites often paint a
detailed picture of a company's technology, pricing, and
future product strategy.

■ ■ ■

SECRETS OF MANUFACTURING

Many manufacturers disassemble their competitors' products. They then price each part, analyzing their competitors' cost of manufacture.[21]

If you plan to manufacture a product, whether radios or hamburgers, you should take apart your competitors' products and price each component. Price everything—from speakers to transistors, from meat to tomatoes.

LABOR COSTS

In many businesses it is the cost of the labor, not the cost of parts, that determines profitability. Calculating the labor content of a product is often difficult. Companies rarely publish detailed financial data on individual products.

Yet by observing your competitors at trade shows, reading their annual reports, visiting their facilities, and counting cars in their parking lots, you can obtain a surprisingly complete picture of how many people were needed to develop, market, and sell a particular product. If you are large enough to have a finance department, ask someone there to calculate your competitors' labor costs. Use this data to benchmark your competitiveness.

■ ■ ■

The Product

■ ■ ■

**Too many technology start-ups
develop a solution
for which there are no customers.**

—Scott A. Ryles, managing director and
head of Global Technology
Investment Banking,
Merrill Lynch

■ ■ ■

Twice in my career I have seen products killed late in the development cycle. One product was finished, worked well, and was ready to ship, but it had no market. The second product had run millions over budget and had been "80% complete" for almost a year. These diverse failures, which occurred at different companies and years apart, had one similarity: The executives involved could not agree on the product's objectives.

Without clearly defined objectives, projects lose their way. Dates slip, costs escalate, and stress mounts. Engineering blames marketing and marketing blames the customer. Yet management itself is often the culprit. In their desire to create a great product—the perfect product—they add ever more features.

This cramming of more and more function into a product is appropriately called "feature-bloat." Simplicity and elegance are its initial victims. As the project slips behind schedule, managers add new people, and the original product vision becomes lost. The lack of shared vision mires the project into a morass of bickering—and ultimately dooms it to failure.

The following questions are deliberately simple—deceptively simple. They force you to create an uncomplicated and enduring vision for your product.

Gain consensus on questions presented in this chapter and you may succeed. Lose consensus on these basics, and you will fail.

Why Would Anyone Buy Your Product?

WHAT VALUE WILL YOU PROVIDE?

Your primary business is to provide value to your customers. If you are unsure what benefits you provide (or which ones are important to your customers), you will lose focus.

Companies uncertain about the value they provide cannot define their objectives. They drift aimlessly from project to project, never quite sure what business they are in. Success eludes them.

Make sure your company is focused by defining your product's objectives below.

My product provides these benefits:

1.

2.

3.

Customers will buy my product because

■ ■ ■

ANDY'S COMPETITIVE ADVANTAGE

The Silicon Deli continues to attract a loyal following of high-tech professionals. Andy, the proprietor of the Silicon Deli, believes that customers patronize his deli because he has these desirable features:

- Central location
- Fast service
- Sandwiches that do not taste like franchise fast-food

But Andy continues to worry about his competitors. What should he do to strengthen his business? He decides to improve his already quick service by opening "Andy's Express Window."

This street-side window sells Andy's four most popular sandwiches. Pre-made earlier in the day, each sandwich is wrapped in a different color butcher paper. To differentiate Andy's from fast-food chains, he autographs each sandwich. He also installs a Web site to take orders and schedule pick-up times.

Andy's Express Window and its Web site attract new customers. The Silicon Deli sells an additional 100 sandwiches per day. With the same staff, it is grossing an additional $10,000 a month.

By focusing his business on one benefit—speed of service—Andy has expanded his customer base. Understand why people want your product, then focus on satisfying that need.

■ ■ ■

WHAT WILL IT LOOK LIKE?

IF IT IS UGLY, NO ONE WILL BUY IT.

Sketch your product and draw a diagram of how it works. For consumer products and software, this can take many hours. It is a good investment. Simple pictures communicate your vision to your source of funding and eventually to your engineering and marketing teams.[22] This activity will also help identify patentable intellectual property. Attach additional sheets as needed.

Sketch how it should *look*.

Diagram how it should *work*.

THE NEW FAMILY SWING SET

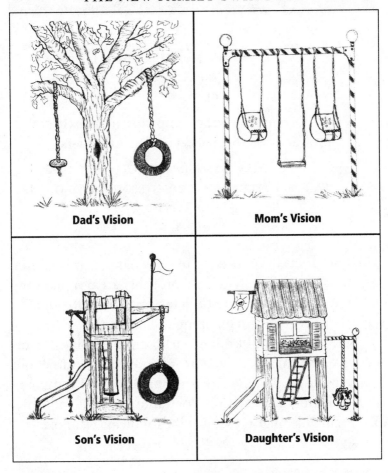

Art by Betsy Grimes

Talking about a new project may create a superficial consensus but miss important details. Talk alone usually fails to create a shared vision. A simple diagram can bring problems to the surface before they become disasters and help build consensus before you invest time and money.

WHEN WILL IT SHIP?

■ ■ ■

It is important for young companies to quickly get product into the market and to customers.

—SCOTT A. RYLES, MANAGING DIRECTOR AND HEAD
OF GLOBAL TECHNOLOGY INVESTMENT BANKING,
Merrill Lynch

■ ■ ■

Most products have three to ten key dates or milestones. If you have only one date, you probably are not planning enough. If you have more than ten milestones for an individual project, you are planning too much.[23]

Selecting the right milestones for your business is imperative. Get the key players in one room and hammer out what the key milestones are for your business. Keep a one-page schedule for each product and review it monthly. Your schedule might resemble the following example:

Task	Date Complete
Demonstrate Prototype	_____
Test Prototype with Users	_____
Complete Research	_____
Finalize Design	_____
Finish the Product	_____
Field Test	_____
Fix Problems Discovered in Field Test	_____
Ship Product	_____
Available on Store Shelves	_____

■ ■ ■

CUPERTINO E-MAIL'S PRODUCT DELAYS

Cupertino E-Mail's sales in the U.S. continue to grow (see page 43). Its clever method of filtering out unwanted e-mail has become quite popular and distributors are calling from Europe and Asia asking for versions supporting additional languages. Cupertino E-Mail's development team attempts to respond by juggling a dozen projects at once. Management moves engineers between projects weekly and things spiral out of control.

They hire an outside consultant who imposes a new planning methodology. Each engineer develops detailed schedules, task lists, and resource requirements for every module. Engineering output falls as everyone is now working on task lists and resource estimates.

Cupertino E-Mail fires the consultant and reverts to its old system of one-page master schedules for each project (see opposite page). It reemphasizes personal and team accountability for making dates, but leaves the details to the individual teams.

To manage its overall business, which now ships five or more products a year, Cupertino E-Mail instigates a one-page master plan. Updated monthly, it tracks final ship dates and major milestones for all projects:

Q1	Q2	Q3	Q4
U.S. Rel 2.0		U.S. Rel 2.1	
	German 1.0		French 1.0
		Spanish Beta	

■ ■ ■

How Different Are You from the Competition?

HOW DO YOU STACK UP?

Make a list of the seven to ten key features and attributes most important to your product's success. Build the list thoughtfully. Your competitors' advertising, Web sites, and packaging may help crystallize your thinking. If the feature list grows beyond twelve, group the list into four or five categories.

Evaluate your product concept against the competitive products. Grade each line item from A to F. You should not beat the competition in every category. This exercise helps you identify your product's unique qualities. Price? Speed? Quality of service? Something else?

For products in new or emerging markets, the competition may be in another, older industry sector. For example, if you are designing a pay-per-view cable TV system, the competition may be video rentals, existing cable TV, and cineplex movie theaters. The following matrix works for PC software and most high-tech products. Modify it to suit your business. Location and visual appeal are important for many businesses and should be on their lists. For service industries—from muffler shops to dry cleaners—speed of service usually replaces throughput (typical time to complete a task). Price should be on everyone's list.

Sample High-Tech Feature Matrix

Key Features	Competitors		Existing Process[1]	You
	A	B		
Price				
Reliability[2]				
Ease of Use[3]				
Ease of Installation[4]				
Ease of Maintenance				
Hidden Costs[5]				
Hardware Prerequisites[6]				
Throughput[7]				

1. The existing process can be a manual process, an old technology, or partially automated process using a competitor's product.
2. Reliability for hardware is usually measured as the mean time to failure. For software this is usually a measure of stability (frequency of crashes) or incompatibility (what products cause crashes when run together).
3. Ease of use is often measured as the time it takes an average user to learn the basic features of the product.
4. Ease of installation is usually measured as the time it takes an average user to install, or the percent of users who successfully install the product without assistance.
5. Hidden costs can be maintenance, upgrade charges, or the cost of supplies.
6. Hardware prerequisites include requirements for memory, hard disk, CPU, or other features.
7. Throughput is the total time it takes a typical person to accomplish a task. For example, how long it takes to type, correct, address, and send an e-mail.

■　■　■

People who say, "I have thought of it, therefore it is a great idea" are the most vulnerable. You must assume someone is already doing it.

—ROY L. ROGERS,
Rogers Investment Corp.

■　■　■

SHOULD YOU DO
PRODUCT SIMULATIONS?

Engineering: "We have this idea for a cool product. . . ."

Marketing: "That doesn't sound very useful."

Engineering: "But it would be very cool, you would get addicted to it once you used it. Give us $2 million and six months and you'll see. . . ."

How do you assess the "coolness factor," or the addictive quality of a new product or feature? Sometimes you have to build it, but frequently that is not necessary. Often you can find a way to simulate the user experience without building the product.

There are several clever ways to do this, including the following methods:

Paper and ink. Carefully draw pictures of all the states of your product. The tester "uses the product" and you quickly switch pictures as though you were the product.

PC simulations. There are numerous products that can simulate PC software and consumer products on a PC screen. Often the simplest simulator is the best. The key is creating an experience that will feel like the finished product.

Phone simulations. Some products (such as tape machines and voice response units) can be simulated by a person on the phone or an audio card in a PC.

■ ■ ■

CONCEPT VIDEOS AND IBM'S VOICE RECOGNITION INVESTMENTS

By 1992, IBM had spent twenty years researching speech recognition without developing commercial products. Many of the key researchers wanted to build commercial products, but they were unable to raise the money. The project was technically risky and expensive. It was unclear whether there was a real market.

Fortuitously, John Scully, then president of Apple, went on *Good Morning America* and showed voice recognition on a Macintosh. His demonstration showed how speech recognition would be used to pay bills and schedule meetings. Simultaneous to the Apple announcement, another IBMer and I produced a "concept video." This very low-budget video was created on an 8-mm camcorder and edited on my home VCR.

These videotapes energized IBM's executives, propelling them into action.

Competitors' videos and your own concept videos can help you crystallize your product vision and obtain funding.

■ ■ ■

WHAT IS
THE PRODUCT'S NAME?

FIND A NAME EARLY

In 1993, I was trying to persuade an IBM executive to introduce a new speech recognition product. He asked what the name would be. I was not thinking about a name since it was six months before the product's earliest possible introduction.

I was naive.

Start working on your name nine to twelve months before you announce your product. The right name will help you raise money, focus your team, and sell your product. The wrong name or no name can be very damaging.

The following process is helpful:

1. Assemble a naming committee of four to six people, including an engineer and a potential user.
2. Brainstorm a list of potential names. Do not evaluate the names—just build the longest possible list of potential names. This process usually yields 50 to 100 candidates.
3. Include all types of names: made-up words, descriptive names, numbers, and acronyms.
4. Give every member five votes and compile the list of the top ten candidates.
5. Have your lawyer do a name search on the favorites. Keep the whole list, as your top choices may all be taken.

■ ■ ■

BRAND IMAGE

Naming can be quite complex. Here are several issues to consider that may affect your brand's image:

Quality Assurance

Companies with advanced product testing and
quality assurance programs frequently pick names
without testing them. The wrong name can lead
to a product's demise. Test the name you've se-
lected in the target market before you ship your
product.

Product Versus Company Name

Sony and BMW use their company names as their
brand; Matsushita and Procter & Gamble do not.
Some companies do both. Again, the watchword
is testing.

Geography and History

The attributes associated with a company or brand
often vary widely between countries. Once a name
is associated with a failure, consider dropping
it. For example, PC Jr. was a great name yet IBM
wisely dropped it.

Uniqueness

Names have unique meaning. They cannot mean
two things simultaneously. Toyota and Honda
dropped their corporate brand in favor of Lexus
and Acura. The old names meant affordable reliability. The new names mean reliable luxury.[24]

■ ■ ■

The Customer

■ ■ ■

**It is so easy to get
wrapped up in your product
and forget all about the customer.**

—DALE L. FULLER, PRESIDENT AND CEO,
WhoWhere? Inc.

■ ■ ■

Recently a major Silicon Valley company invited me to attend their annual executive planning session.

Most of the executives and several of the engineers around the table were multimillionaires since the company's stock and the employees' options had done extraordinarily well.

Mid-morning on the second day, the topic of the customer's needs came up. One senior executive observed, "We have been discussing the technical details of what to build for almost two days, and this is the first time anyone has asked what the customer wants."

This is an almost universal problem in high-tech companies. Marketing, engineering, and executive management become so enamored with the technology that they lose sight of the customer.

Sometimes customers cannot tell you their needs. To borrow from Daniel Burrus, author of *Technotrends,* few housewives knew they needed self-cleaning ovens before they were invented.

Often the technology creates the need. Nevertheless, you need to stay close to your customer and not fall into the trap of obsessing on the technology.

Whether you are building a revolutionary, groundbreaking product or opening a coffee shop, you should talk with your future customers. Show them pictures or drawings of the product and the packaging. Ask them whether they would buy from you. Ask them what would improve the product. Listen carefully to their answers.

Ignore your customer and you may spend millions developing the wrong product.

DO THE CUSTOMERS THINK IT IS A GOOD IDEA?

■ ■ ■

No business is a business without customers.

—SCOTT A. RYLES, MANAGING DIRECTOR AND HEAD
OF GLOBAL TECHNOLOGY INVESTMENT BANKING,
Merrill Lynch

■ ■ ■

Early in the design cycle, before you have invested much time and money, talk with your potential customers. Show them your hand-drawn picture of the product. Ask them, "Would you buy this product?" "How much would you pay for it?" Listen carefully to their answers and take notes.

Customer number one thinks:

Customer number two thinks:

Customer number three thinks:

■ ■ ■

THE PALO ALTO PC COMPANY

During the previous five years, the Palo Alto PC Company had captured a significant percentage of the notebook PC market. They had built a strong network of distributors by marketing to corporate customers. Their PCs were smaller and better looking than many of those offered by their Taiwanese competitors. They commanded a premium price.

As Palo Alto PC began designing their fourth generation notebook, they did a cursory survey of their largest distributors. They assumed, and their distributors confirmed, that "Customers want it even smaller."

The new Palo Alto PC notebook was a hit with the media. Its innovative keyboard made it both small and cute. Unfortunately, few customers bought it. Sales plummeted. It turns out that executives wanted longer battery life, brighter screens, and thinner PCs—but not smaller keyboards.

How did the Palo Alto PC Company lose their way so quickly? They forgot who the real customer was. They acted as though the distributors were their customers. Customers are the people who ultimately buy and use the product.

Distributors are helpful, but they are not ultimate users of your product. Distributors will tell you what customers wanted last month; users will tell you what they want today.

■ ■ ■

WHO IS THE <u>REAL</u> CUSTOMER?

HOW BIG IS YOUR <u>REAL</u> MARKET?

Clearly define your target customers. Do they exhibit specific buying habits? Is a prerequisite required? The more comprehensive the definition of your customer, the more likely you will succeed. For example, consider the customers in Question 2 and then define further:

The Customer	Prerequisites and Environment
Users of Windows 95	Owning a joystick
Viewers of the home shopping channel	Buying children's clothing costing more than $45
Homeowners painting their homes	Needing exterior stains
Teenage boys, 16–18 years old	Buying athletic shoes for over $100

The buyers of my product have these prerequisites or exhibit these buying habits:

1.

2.

3.

■ ■ ■

THE FLOWER CART DECIDES "EVERYONE" IS THEIR CUSTOMER

Flush with success, the flower cart owner (page 11) dreams of supplying corporate customers and weddings, as well as commuters. She rents a store across the street from the train station, increases inventory, starts to advertise, and fails.

Less than two minutes from the old location, the new store is more expensive to operate yet generates less revenue. The reason: It lacks focus. The flower cart had been successful because it targeted commuters who:

1. Were reminded of flowers just when they were starting to think of their families

2. Could see their train on the tracks and knew they still had time to shop

The new flower store targets everyone but pleases no one.

Paradoxically, focusing on a narrow target market may increase your sales elsewhere because this focus gives your business a personality to which buyers can relate. Targeting "everyone" in your city or country will increase your costs. Focusing on a narrow segment of buyers usually increases sales and conserves cash.

■ ■ ■

WHAT ARE
YOUR CUSTOMERS' SECRETS?

RESEARCH YOUR CUSTOMERS AS THOROUGHLY AS YOU RESEARCH YOUR COMPETITORS

The techniques used to uncover your competitors' secrets should also be used to research your customers.[25] In summary, these include research through:

- A local library
- The Web
- Want ads
- Customer interviews
- Search services
- Trade shows

Additionally, ask yourself, "What do my potential customers have in common?" If they are all in the same industry, there is probably an industry association. If they are in the same city, county, or state, there will be a chamber of commerce. If they are in a foreign country, there will be a trade officer at the embassy[26] and often a locally sponsored trade development council or board.

These groups are usually a wealth of statistical data. They will often meet with you and arrange introductions with potential customers, distributors, and business partners.

■ ■ ■

HOW WELL DO YOU KNOW YOUR CUSTOMERS?

Score the first three questions as follows:
Do not know = 0
Have a good guess = 5
Definitely know = 10

Score

Age Demographics
Percentage under age 20, between
20 and 30, etc. This is important even
when you sell to corporations. ____

Income Level
Personal income for consumer
products, company sales for corporate
products. ____

Method of Payment
Percentage of buyers using credit
cards, cash, or purchase orders. ____

Sex
5 points for the buyer and 5 points
for the user. ____

Current Suppliers
3 points if you can name them,
10 points if you know their
market share. ____

TOTAL ____

How You Scored:
45 to 50 Too good to be true, unless this is a
new release of an existing product
36 to 44 Experienced product manager
25 to 35 MBA graduate
Under 25 Just starting out

■ ■ ■

SHOULD YOU DO
FOCUS GROUPS?

READ THE SCRIPT BEFOREHAND
AND ATTEND THE FIRST SESSION

Focus groups are usually run by a professional moderator who interviews groups of six to ten people. They provide consumer feedback on a wide variety of topics including:

- New product concepts
- Competitors' products
- Consumers' usage patterns
- Consumers' feelings about products
- Packaging, advertising, and promotions

Focus groups can be helpful and they can be misleading.[27] To have a successful focus group, follow these guidelines: First, collect demographic and statistical data about your customers and competitors. Then hire an experienced, professional moderator. And finally, develop a concise, specific description of the information you want from a focus group:

A focus group will tell us more about

■ ■ ■

THE TALKING COOKBOOK

Pierre, the head chef at the Palo Alto Boheme Restaurant, wants to develop an electronic kitchen assistant. He envisions an interactive CD that talks to the novice French cook, verbally coaching them through each step of a recipe. He finds several wealthy patrons to back his new enterprise and hires Henry, a recent MBA graduate, to develop the business plan.

Henry quickly develops a prototype and things proceed smoothly until their first focus group. The prototype receives positive reviews; unfortunately no one in the focus group has a PC in their kitchen. While everyone likes it, no one expresses interest in buying it. Several people spontaneously suggest a self-contained kitchen appliance with voice recognition.

Unfortunately, a self-contained unit would cost almost $1,000 to build. Pierre is irate, angry at Henry, and angry at the focus group.

Henry suggests a small wireless intercom that sits in the kitchen and communicates with the PC. This can be built for under $100. Henry convenes a new focus group and the modified design passes with flying colors.

As Pierre discovered, focus groups can uncover the flaws in business plans before they become disasters.

■ ■ ■

HOW MUCH
WILL THE CUSTOMER PAY?

ASK THEM

Predicting how much customers will pay for a product or service is often difficult. If products similar to yours already exist, the guidelines in Question 6 should help you. But if you have a "first in category" or revolutionary product, you will need to interview your potential customers and your sales channel.

The following exercise is always helpful: Interview four or more customers, asking each one how much he or she would pay for your product. Also interview several of your colleagues, asking them how much the product should cost and why.

Customer #1:	Your Engineers:
Customer #2:	Your Sales Team:
Customer #3:	Your Distributors:
Customer #4:	Your Instincts:

■ ■ ■

PORTOLA HILLS SOFTWARE

My friend George retired early from Intel and became the Director of Business Development at a small company, Portola Hills Software. For the previous five years, the company had been a contract programming shop. They rented programmers to larger companies for $75 to $200 per hour. Much of their business came from developing software that improved the yields in semiconductor manufacturing.

The allure of higher margins seduced Portola Hills Software's owners to enter the software business. They borrowed $3 million, brought their programmers in-house and started to build the world's best semiconductor process control software. George joined Portola Hills Software two years into its transformation.

On George's first day on the job, he asked to see the business plan. There was an expense plan, a hiring plan, and a product plan; that was it. Portola Hills Software had never seriously talked dollars and dates with their potential customers.

Over the next few months, George visited every major semiconductor company in the world. There was no interest in the product. Semiconductor companies were unwilling to switch from their existing systems.

Portola Hills Software declared bankruptcy later that year.

■ ■ ■

The Marketing Strategy

■ ■ ■

Most new companies with innovative products
spend excessive time on product development.
New companies overlook the fact
that products need to be marketed,
sold, and converted to cash.

—WILLIAM M. COCKRUM, PROFESSOR,
Anderson School of Management at UCLA

■ ■ ■

New products rarely jump off the shelves by themselves. Many young engineers have watched in frustration as their creations have failed because of poor marketing. Similarly, many entrepreneurs spend 90% of their time and money on their product, ignoring sales and marketing, only to fail due to a lack of customers.

Marketing counts. Great products deserve great marketing and mediocre products need great marketing. Whether your product is revolutionary or mundane, you need to develop a marketing strategy. Doing so may uncover flaws in your product or packaging, and such planning will usually impress your investors.

Developing an effective marketing program is difficult. There is an almost infinite number of ways to market a product. For example, you might use:

- Discount coupons
- Dealer awards
- Flyers
- Brochures
- New packaging
- Frequent-user programs
- Newspaper advertisements
- Trade shows
- Sales incentives
- In-store displays
- Mailings
- Catalogs
- Tele-sales programs
- Web pages
- Customer briefings

Developing great marketing programs, like developing great products, demands that you focus on a small number of items that will result in the success of your product or business.

How do you find the right marketing programs for your product? The next seven questions will provide helpful strategies.

WHAT IS
YOUR STRATEGIC OBJECTIVE?

WHAT DEFINES SUCCESS?

A strategic objective provides direction to your business and a yardstick by which you can measure your success and the success of your marketing programs. A strategic objective typically has three components: a product, a time frame, and a measurable target. For example:

Strategic Objective	Product	Time Frame	Target
Put our collision avoidance system in every car by 2010	Collision avoidance system	By 2010	100% market share
Grow revenue 15% a year	All products	Open-ended, forever	15% revenue growth
Fastest Web server within two years	Internet Web server	Next two years	Faster than competitors

What Is Your:

Strategic Objective	Product	Time Frame	Target

WHAT ARE YOUR PERSONAL OBJECTIVES?

Some hardworking entrepreneurs behave as though their personal objective is to work 60-hour weeks until they have a heart attack. This dysfunctional behavior hurts their businesses as well as their families.

There is an interrelationship between your personal and business objectives. Individuals with strong personal goals are more effective at launching new products and businesses. Effective personal objectives usually have a target and a time frame.

Examples of personal objectives:

- Start my own business in the next 10 years.
- Retire at age 55 and travel 3 months each year.
- Acquire enough stock options in a successful company to quit and become a teacher.

Develop a short definition of where you want to be in 10 years.

My personal objective is

WHAT IS YOUR MARKETING OBJECTIVE?

■ ■ ■

One of the biggest challenges of a small company is to create mind share.

—SCOTT A. RYLES, MANAGING DIRECTOR AND HEAD
OF GLOBAL TECHNOLOGY INVESTMENT BANKING,
Merrill Lynch

■ ■ ■

Many companies fail to identify their marketing objective. They have a sales objective or strategic objective and assume these are their marketing objectives. Unlike a sales objective, which is measured in revenue, a marketing objective focuses on changing people's perceptions and behavior.

While a strategic objective may remain fixed, marketing objectives will change as the product and its competitive climate mature. Which of the following is most important to your success?

☐ Persuade users of the *need* for a product like yours.

☐ Raise *awareness of your product* and its name.

☐ Sell the *benefits of your product.*

☐ Encourage *new customers* to try it.

☐ Encourage *existing customers* to buy more.

TEST YOUR MARKETING SAVVY

Match the boxes on the right with the boxes on the left.

MARKETING PROGRAM	THE OBJECTIVE
TV ad campaign ☐ "Listerine Kills Germs"	☐ **Need:** Persuade users of the need for the product.
A billboard for a ☐ congressional race	☐ **Awareness:** Raise the awareness of the product and its name.
A Web site with ☐ product specifications	☐ **Benefits:** Sell the benefits of the product.
A $50 rebate for a ☐ bread maker	
TV ad campaign[28] ☐ Alka-Seltzer's "Plop plop fizz fizz" ads	☐ **New Customers:** Encourage new customers to try the product.
Loyalty program ☐ American Airline's frequent flyer points	☐ **Existing Customers:** Encourage existing customers to buy more.
Affinity credit card[29] ☐ GM's VISA card	

(Answers are on page 141.)

How Will You Sell and Support the Product?

HOW DO YOU SIMPLIFY THE BUYING PROCESS?

Some Internet software companies build products, issue press releases, and watch the world beat a path to their Web site. But most companies need a plan to market, distribute, sell, and support their product.

A channel strategy describes how you will accomplish these nonengineering tasks. This strategy encompasses all the tasks required to market, sell, and distribute a product. These seemingly unrelated activities are surprisingly interrelated. Change your distribution strategy, and you may have to change your packaging or rethink your technical support plan.

Many companies have multiple channels of product distribution as part of their overall strategy. For example, Intuit sells its software through 800 numbers and retail channels. And most companies have different channel strategies for different countries.

It pays to worry about these issues. As much as 80% of the money customers pay for your product may go to sales, marketing, distribution, support, and dealer discounts. Design a more effective and efficient way to do these tasks, and you can pocket the money you save.

THE CHANNEL STRATEGY

Have you thought through the nuances of your marketing and logistics plan? Who will inventory, market, advertise, and support your product? Give each key area of responsibility its own box, then:

1. Put a name in each box.
2. Add additional boxes as needed.
3. Draw arrows between boxes.

Most companies develop specific channel strategies for each product or family of related products. A channel strategy should be comprehensive and may grow to more than a dozen boxes including items such as proposal preparation, pricing, and tele-sales.

Marketing Programs, and Advertising:	Artwork, Packaging, and Manuals:
Dealer Promotions:	**Manufacturing:**
Customer Support:	**Inventory Management:**
Distribution and Delivery:	**The Buyer:**
Sales:	**The End User:**

WHO WILL GENERATE DEMAND?

HOW WILL YOU PRESENT THE BENEFITS OF YOUR PRODUCT TO THE USER?

The physical distribution and "shelf stocking" of your product is not the key element of a channel strategy; demand generation is.

Draw lines from one or more boxes on the left to one or more boxes on the right. Use thick lines to represent major thrusts, thin lines for secondary efforts. The best solutions often have only one or two lines:

Who Will Generate Demand?		*How* Will They Generate Demand?	
You	☐	☐	Print, TV, or Radio Ads
Your Partners	☐	☐	Phone Calls or Mailings
Your Salespeople	☐	☐	Through the Internet
A Distributor	☐	☐	Prominent Location
A Manufacturer's Representative[30]	☐	☐	Eye-Catching Packaging
		☐	Presentations or Seminars
Retail Store	☐	☐	Other _____
Other _____	☐		

■ ■ ■

COMMON MISCONCEPTIONS:

Distributors will spend their money on advertising.

Rarely. Distributors will spend *your* money on advertising.

Another division will sell the product.

It never works, unless your product can contribute more than 20% to their bottom line. Another division will charge you 25–60% to distribute your product, but will rarely commit in writing to substantial marketing and advertising dollars.

Foreign distributors are not important.

Foreign distributors can double your revenue. Hire a bright MBA from a U.S. business school who grew up in your primary foreign market. Allocate 20–60% of your marketing and sales budget to international markets.[31]

Hire the sales team right before the product launch.

It is very risky to wait this long. It can take six months or more to hire and train salespeople.

■ ■ ■

WILL YOU NEED MARKETING OR SALES?

Most organizations need both sales and marketing. Marketing and sales require different skills that are not interchangeable. A few brief job descriptions may help you identify what you really need. Smaller organizations often combine the first three sales functions into one business development position and the latter three positions into one product marketing position.

Sales Representatives or Sales Executives spend most of their time selling to customers. They have territories, quotas, commissions, bonuses, and make lots of money.

The Manager of Business Development sells things that do not yet exist but you are considering developing.

The Channel Manager or Channel Sales Executive sells to your indirect channels: VARs,[32] dealers, and distributors.

The Public Relations Manager manages the press. This may seem extravagant, but it is critical for IPOs (Initial Public Offerings).

The Product Manager is the primary liaison with manufacturing and engineering. The individual in this position manages product requirements, packaging, manuals, and logistics.[33]

The Marketing Manager is responsible for almost everything else, including product introductions, trade shows, and advertising.

■ ■ ■

HOW MUCH SHOULD YOU SPEND ON MARKETING AND SALES?[34]

Some products need large advertising budgets to succeed; others require guerrilla marketing. Answer the following questions to determine which you need.

	No	Yes
Consumer Product? Will individual consumers make the buying decision?	☐	☐
New Type of Product? Does it satisfy a new need?	☐	☐
Addictive Product? Do users really like the product once they use it?	☐	☐
Brand Names? Will more than 50% of sales go to name brands in 5 years?	☐	☐
High Volumes Required? Do you need to sell over 100,000 units to become profitable?	☐	☐
Critical Mass? Do you have over 100 employees?	☐	☐
TOTALS	___	___

Scoring:

Three or more answered "No": Conserve your cash. Use guerrilla marketing or hire a small sales team.

Four or more answered "Yes": This product probably needs a serious advertising budget.

■ ■ ■

What Is the Marketing Plan?

■ ■ ■

History teaches that the only thing that works in marketing is the single, bold stroke. . . .

—Al Ries and Jack Trout, authors
of *The Twenty-Two Immutable Laws of Marketing*
(HarperCollins, 1994)

■ ■ ■

Assemble a small group to brainstorm and build a list of potential marketing programs. Don't evaluate the ideas; don't critique them; don't price them.[35] Just build a list of 20 to 60 possible programs. Then sort them into three categories: "A-list" things to do in the first 6 months; "B-list" things to do in the first year; and "C-list" things to do later (maybe).

Limit your "A-list" to 12 items maximum.

Some examples would be:

A Write Press release

A Write Technical Fact Sheet

A Call your 20 largest potential customers

A Call 5 potential distributors

B Attend an industry trade show[36]

B Run distributor technical training

B Hire a marketing manager

C Develop a magazine advertising campaign

■ ■ ■

MARKETING RESCUES THE SILICON VALLEY REPERTORY THEATER

Silicon Valley's Repertory Theater was floundering. A typical performance lasted 2½ hours, required twelve volunteers, and attracted fewer than twenty theatergoers. The organization was delinquent in its payments to the local community center for the use of its 1,500-seat theater. A sad situation.

Your first instinct may be to either "downsize" the theater or just blow it up. Before you pull out the knife on a hopeless money-loser, try brainstorming with the key players. Use the technique outlined on the previous pages. Host three sessions—one focused on marketing, one on the finances, and one on the product or service.

Brainstorming often yields surprisingly innovative potential solutions, such as the following:

- Raising the price of tickets from $8 to $35 dollars, moving to a very small theater and making the tickets difficult to get.

- Hosting fund-raisers for nonprofits one night a week.

- Renting a restaurant normally closed on Saturday afternoon, creating a luncheon showing.

- Putting the first act on the Web.

■ ■ ■

HOW DO YOU BECOME FRONT PAGE NEWS?

■ ■ ■

Successful start-ups manage the media.

—SCOTT A. RYLES, MANAGING DIRECTOR AND HEAD
OF GLOBAL TECHNOLOGY INVESTMENT BANKING,
Merrill Lynch

■ ■ ■

Imagine the story of your new business or product becoming a big success. Now write the story that would appear in the *Wall Street Journal.*

Format the story so it looks real. This powerful technique ties the whole marketing and technical story together by forcing you to explain your ideas in simple-to-understand language. This approach conveys your vision and can help you obtain funding.[37]

Later, when you start building your business, this technique will help you craft the key messages for press interviews and marketing collateral.

If you are part of a larger organization, write a second article, in which your product was not funded. Focus on the success of a competitor and the strategic impact on your parent company. In larger enterprises, projects may be funded to protect the company's core business.

■ ■ ■

FOR IMMEDIATE RELEASE: L'CHEF REVOLUTIONIZES FRENCH COOKING

WORLD'S FIRST TALKING KITCHEN ASSISTANT

LAS VEGAS, Nev.—Palo Alto Boheme, Inc., unveiled L'Chef, the world's first talking kitchen assistant. Retailing for under $200, L'Chef talks the aspiring home chef through the subtleties of French cooking.

L'Chef resembles a mouse and uses a patented wireless technology to communicate between the kitchen and a home PC. The mouse's tail is actually an antenna.

After selecting a recipe on a PC, L'Chef talks the home cook through the recipe. Stylishly engineered, L'Chef's five buttons—Pause, Help, Backup, Skip, and Start Again—enable both novice and expert to produce extraordinary cuisine.

"The microprocessor will revolutionize the kitchen," said world-renowned French chef turned innovator, Pierre d'Coutre, who demonstrated L'Chef at the Consumer Electronics Show in Las Vegas (booth 21055). . . .

(For more information on drafting press releases see the Anatomy of a Press Release on pages 136–138.)

■ ■ ■

CHAPTER EIGHT

Confronting the Truth

■ ■ ■

The best way to make a lot of money
in a new venture . . .
is to be ruthlessly honest
about the real risks in the business.

—JOHN DOERR, PARTNER,
Kleiner Perkins Caufield & Byers, from *Going Global*
by William C. Taylor and Alan M. Webber

■ ■ ■

My second-grade Irish nun was fond of saying, "God sends you little warning signals when bad things are about to happen." Whether sent by God or not, disasters do have warning signals.

Many businesspeople undervalue their intuition, incorrectly assuming their instincts are wrong and the data is right. This is naive. If you have a bad feeling about something, assume there is a problem.

When IBM was announcing its first speech dictation system, the *Wall Street Journal* sent a writer to review the software. The meeting and demonstration went well, but something kept bothering me. After multiple follow-up phone calls, we discovered that the journalist was writing a negative article because we had not allowed him to write his article using the new software. We arranged for this to happen and got a good review in the *Journal.*[38]

We had flirted with disaster. The resulting half-page article appeared on the front page of the *Wall Street Journal's* second section, which is widely read in high-tech circles. Had the story been negative, it would have killed the first product and perhaps the whole product line.

Computers, color charts, and statistics are all useful, but they are recent inventions and people are still figuring out how to use them. Human instincts have evolved over ten millennia and saved countless lives. When a warning bell goes off in your brain, stop, pay attention, and listen to your feelings.

Is This the Right Project for You?

WHY ARE YOU DOING THIS?

Starting a new business, building a new product, or changing companies is a major commitment. If you have to leave your current job to start your new one, you are actually making two decisions simultaneously. Should you really quit your current job? Is this the right next step for you? Before you take the plunge talk with:

- ☐ friends
- ☐ relatives
- ☐ colleagues
- ☐ potential customers
- ☐ a future competitor
- ☐ someone who has already left your current situation.

My motivation for change is

■ ■ ■

WHY DO PEOPLE BECOME ENTREPRENEURS?

GORDON MOORE, cofounder of Intel, was asked what motivated him to leave Fairchild Semiconductor and start Intel. Here is part of his response:

> I was getting somewhat frustrated because it was increasingly difficult to get our new ideas into the company's products. As the company grew, it became more and more difficult to transfer the ideas and the new technology. (*San Jose Mercury News,* January 26, 1997)

■ ■ ■

SCOTT MCNEALY was similarly asked about his inspiration for founding Sun Microsystems. His reply:

> I didn't like my boss. (*San Jose Mercury News,* January 27, 1997)

■ ■ ■

WHAT IS YOUR CORE COMPETENCY?

A NEW BUSINESS SUCCEEDS BY FOCUSING

What skills are critical to your success? What will make your business or product unique? What do you enjoy doing?

Check as few of the following boxes as possible:

Research, Design, and Manufacturing
- ☐ Mathematics and Algorithms
- ☐ Quick Design
- ☐ Innovative Features
- ☐ Ease of Use
- ☐ Low-Cost Manufacturing

Sales and Marketing
- ☐ Large Account Sales
- ☐ Advertising
- ☐ In-Store Merchandising

Distribution and General Business
- ☐ Building Alliances
- ☐ Physical Distribution
- ☐ Import or Export
- ☐ Land Acquisition
- ☐ Franchising
- ☐ Creative Financing
- ☐ Electronic Sales Via the Internet
- ☐ Other _____

■ ■ ■

AT&T AND EO

AT&T's EO subsidiary tried to build a new revolutionary computer notebook without a keyboard. EO had 200 employees working on dozens of different components: a new operating system, new fax software, revolutionary hardware, a new AT&T chip (the Hobbit), and an advanced handwriting recognition system. The device ultimately cost too much, and AT&T pulled the plug.[39]

Paradoxically, EO was so innovative it had no identifiable competitive advantage.

Trying to Do Everything Yourself?

While striving for perfection, entrepreneurs often try to do everything. They fail to focus on their competitive advantage. Perfectionists, they dislike using subcontractors. Visionaries, they eschew standard parts, designing everything from scratch.

These entrepreneurs' inability to identify and focus on their key competitive advantage inevitably causes problems. Costs increase and products are late. While trying to do too much, they find their cash running short and bankruptcy may follow.

■ ■ ■

WILL THE BUSINESS WORK?

TRUTHFULLY, CAN YOU DELIVER?

Behind most failures is a lack of truthfulness. Entrepreneurs who are enthusiastic about their business deceive themselves. This lack of candor seems to be concentrated in four areas. Scrutinize a failed business, and inevitably you will find too much optimism about one or more of these four elements of the business plan.

Whether you are analyzing your own business plans or auditing someone else's, carefully examine these four questions:

1. How much will it cost to build?　$ _____

2. How much will customers pay?　$ _____

3. Will the product work? Can you deliver the key features and benefits you have promised?

   Definitely ☐　　Maybe ☐

4. Does anyone really need the product?

   Definitely ☐　　Maybe ☐

■ ■ ■

SUNNYVALE SERVER'S BANKRUPTCY

Sunnyvale Server manufactured highly reliable—and highly priced—servers for local area networks (LANs). Founded by several well-known Valley entrepreneurs, the company had three years of explosive growth followed by two years of intense competition. Last year they surprised their customers and employees when they declared bankruptcy.

At a recent Woodside cocktail party, their vice president of engineering commented on the demise:

"We missed three of the basics. First, we could never build the product cheaply enough. We couldn't compete with high-end PCs.

"Second, we were never able to deliver the key functions we promised our customers. We promised them 24-hour availability, and it was impossible to deliver.

"And finally, '24-hour availability' was a great marketing spiel, but it turns out most customers didn't really need it.

"We blew the basics. We were wrong about our costs, wrong about customers needs, and wrong about how much function we could really deliver."

■ ■ ■

WOULD YOUR ENGINEERS BUY THE PRODUCT?

■ ■ ■

If the idea for a new instrument appealed to the HP engineer working at the next bench, it would very likely appeal to our customers as well.

—DAVID PACKARD in *The HP Way*.
(HarperCollins Publishers, 1995)

■ ■ ■

Recently I visited a large manufacturing facility. Engineering, marketing, manufacturing, and the executive suites were all in the same building. The manufacturing "clean rooms" could be viewed through glass walls on the way to the company cafeteria.

The marketing executive was showing me the preproduction prototypes of various products, some of which had become enormously profitable and others that had failed.

As we sat there, with the products displayed in front of us, the marketing executive made one of the most profoundly useful statements in the history of product development, "Products we like are not necessarily successful, but products that we don't like in-house never succeed with customers." If your marketing and engineering teams don't want the product, it will not succeed.

■ ■ ■

IBM'S SPEECH TEAM

At the peak of its development efforts in the mid-90s, IBM had 120 people doing research, development, and marketing for speech recognition products. Initially only two of the 120 used IBM speech products themselves. Everyone had an opinion on how customers would use the products, but no one used the products at home or in the office.[40]

I should have recognized this as a major warning signal, and questioned: What is so wrong with a product that 118 of the people most familiar with it do not use it?

Hundreds of high-tech companies fall into this trap. They discourage the employees directly responsible for a product from using it at work and at home. Concerned about cost and confidentiality, they pass up thousands of free hours of user testing.

If you are considering investing your time or money in a consumer product, observe those most familiar with it. If the engineers do not use it, beware. Something is wrong with the product or with the management team.

■ ■ ■

ARE YOU TELLING YOURSELF THE TRUTH?

■ ■ ■

**The biggest failure I ever participated in
happened because I didn't trust my gut.**

—SCOTT A. RYLES, MANAGING DIRECTOR AND HEAD
OF GLOBAL TECHNOLOGY INVESTMENT BANKING,
Merrill Lynch

■ ■ ■

Your intuition may tell you what the numbers cannot. Periodically take a moment and check your instincts.

Imagine you have just opened your business or shipped your product. Try to visualize the future. Instinctively, but truthfully, grade the following statements from A to F:

☐ The product will work well.

☐ The product will sell well.

☐ The business will be a financial success.

☐ I will enjoy the day-to-day management of this project.

☐ I will be better off financially than I am now.

☐ I will have better career prospects than I do now.

☐ My family will be happier.

☐ I can exit the deal easily if it doesn't work.

■ ■ ■

CHIP'S LIMITED PARTNERSHIP

Chip loved to fly. A graduate student, he could not afford an airplane nor the cost of lessons for his commercial license. An acquaintance, a physician at Palo Alto Hospital, suggested he form a limited partnership for several doctors. The limited partnership would buy a plane and pay for Chip's lessons. In return, Chip would work as their personal pilot for several years for free.

Three years of flying was seductive, but Chip was not comfortable with some of the fine print in the partnership agreement. Chip wanted to fly and was willing to work, but he did not want to run a mini-airline for a group of doctors.

Chip decided to focus on his real desire—to trade his labor for flight time and lessons. Within two days he found a growing flight school that was looking for someone to answer their phone on Saturdays. The flight school quickly struck a deal with Chip, which saved them money and enabled Chip to fly and earn his commercial license.

Chip's desire to fly was so strong that he almost agreed to three years of indentured servitude. Luckily, he focused on his real desire—flying—and found a situation that truly satisfied his needs without giving up his freedom.[41]

■ ■ ■

Raising Money

■ ■ ■

**No worthwhile venture should fail
because it ran out of money.
If it's a good project,
we ought to be able to get
the capital to fund it.**

—JOHN DOERR, PARTNER,
Kleiner Perkins Caufield & Byers, from *Going Global*
by William C. Taylor and Alan M. Webber.

■ ■ ■

Most organizations have a process for allocating funds to new projects. The neophyte believes that a business plan is the first step in the process. This is rarely true. Most projects have an executive sponsor before they have a business plan.

The written plan performs two diametrically opposed functions. For projects with an executive sponsor, the business planning process creates consensus and develops clear objectives. For projects without an executive sponsor, the preparation of a business plan mires the aspiring entrepreneur in endless paperwork.

Before you write a detailed business plan, talk with other entrepreneurs and executives. Find out who makes investments in your company or in your industry. Then put together a presentation (see page 122) and solicit feedback from them.

Most executives make investment decisions quickly. The idea is appealing or it is not. They may invest many hours nurturing the project—but only if they initially like it. They form their opinions quickly, focusing on the following short list of criteria:

- Is it technically possible to build the product?
- Are the cost targets attainable?
- Is there a real need, a real market, for the product?
- Is there synergy with the executive's core business?

Address these issues succinctly, and you may find an early supporter. Once an executive believes a market is real and the product genuine, he or she will help you find funding.

SHOULD YOU INVEST YOUR OWN MONEY?

CAUTIOUSLY!

Avoid being the only financial backer of a project:

Don't spend your own money on something that no one else in America will invest in.

Ask yourself: Where are all the customers? Who is the channel? Why won't they invest?

If you have financial partners, when things get tough, they will be motivated to help. If you go it alone and run short of cash, you may be in real trouble.

Never:

- Mortgage your house.
- Borrow against your 401k.
- Use your kids' college funds.

If you cannot stop yourself, call your mother, your brother, a Republican relative—anyone conservative.

If the idea is great, someone else will invest in it. If no one else wants to invest in your project, something is wrong. Your guardian angel is trying to tell you that Intel or Microsoft is already developing your product.

■ ■ ■

COUNTERPOINT

Are you in or are you out? Are you committed or are you just on the sidelines?

—JAMES M. COUGHLIN, VICE PRESIDENT AND
GENERAL MANAGER, StarTemps, Inc.

The requirement to put your own money into the deal to get equity varies widely by industry. In the high-tech sector, there is little need for the principals to mortgage their homes.[42] In other industries, owning a piece of the business requires an investment of your money.

Should you invest your own money? I have two suggestions:

1. **Manage someone else's business before you start your own.** Run a McDonald's franchise for a year before you buy one. You may not earn much, but you will learn the business without putting your savings at risk.

2. **Calculate the cost of failure.** Will you have to sell the house? Will you have to put the kids in new schools? Discuss the worst-case scenario with your family. If it's something you can live with, then go for it.

■ ■ ■

WHAT DO YOU SAY TO THE POTENTIAL INVESTORS?

■ ■ ■

Don't get confused and think a venture capitalist cares about you. They care about making money.

—DALE L. FULLER, PRESIDENT AND CEO,
WhoWhere? Inc.

■ ■ ■

Be deferential. Use an extraordinarily respectful tone of voice, but ask the tough questions. He (or she) needs to respect you. You need to know the one with the money and understand when the plug will be pulled.

Practice in front of a mirror. Take this list with you and ask:

1. Have you ever had a deal quite like this one?
2. What do you see as the key milestones in the first year? In the second year?
3. What do you get out of this project?
4. What is your success rate on projects like this?
5. Have you seen or are you investing in any similar ventures?
6. Are you going to support this project?
7. What would cause you to change your mind?[43]

People with money are flattered to be asked for their opinions. Typically, they are just asked for money.

■ ■ ■

THE 3-SENTENCE PROPOSAL

When I come up with a new idea, I usually have an informal conversation with several friends and colleagues. Once I can successfully answer their questions, I broach the subject with an executive who could fund the project. A simple three-sentence business proposition seems to work best. For example:

"George, I have been thinking about a product that would do such and such. I think we could build it for about x dollars. At that cost there might be a significant market."

Then I stop and listen.

Usually I get questions—which is a good sign—or occasionally I see a frown and hear a "Tried that once and it didn't work."

If you get a negative response, do not get emotional. Do keep an open mind and ask questions: "George, you look skeptical" or "What went wrong?" Take notes and do not get angry.

Always close the conversation with, "Are you interested?" If his or her answer is "No," ask who else might be.

■ ■ ■

CAN YOU IMPRESS
A VENTURE CAPITALIST?

■ ■ ■

**Honesty and integrity are an important part of a
relationship between entrepreneurs and a venture
capitalist. It is the absolute starting point.**

—ROY L. ROGERS,
Rogers Investment Corp.

■ ■ ■

Businesses funded by venture capital are more likely to
succeed and yield higher market valuations than businesses funded from other sources.[44] Of the following attributes that impress venture capitalists, which do you possess?

☐ **Customers**   Do you have six or more customers
who have agreed to buy your
product?

☐ **Growing**   Does the data show rapid market
Market   growth?

☐ **Experience**   Do you have relevant business
experience?

☐ **Competitive**   Do you know what your potential
Knowledge   competitors are doing?

☐ **Uniqueness**   Is some aspect of your business—its
technology or location—unique?

■ ■ ■

DO YOU HAVE A DEFENSIBLE COMPETITIVE ADVANTAGE?

Venture capitalists take large financial risks and expect large returns. They look for opportunities to create a unique product that can maintain its uniqueness over time. If it can be copied too quickly, the financial return will be low and the venture unattractive. A unique defensible competitive advantage—along with cost and market demand—is foremost in a venture capitalist's mind.

Does your product have a unique competitive advantage? Can you do one thing better than anyone else in the world? Will you still be best-in-class next year? If you can convince the right people that you have a defensible competitive advantage, you will probably be able to raise money. This does not guarantee a successful business, but it is often sufficient to obtain financing.

Who will be the best-in-class twelve months from now? Compare yourself to three competitors in the following areas. Put only one check per row:

	Competitors			
	A	**B**	**C**	**You**
Patented Technology	☐	☐	☐	☐
Unpatented Designs	☐	☐	☐	☐
Cycle Time	☐	☐	☐	☐
Marketing and Advertising	☐	☐	☐	☐
Salesforce	☐	☐	☐	☐
Low-Cost Manufacturing	☐	☐	☐	☐
Other	☐	☐	☐	☐

■ ■ ■

WHO ARE YOUR FRIENDS?

ASK THEM FOR HELP

In 1992 a colleague and I began to lobby IBM to take its speech recognition technology out of research and develop commercial products. We talked with dozens of IBM managers and executives.

The typical response was, "It's not my job to worry about this." Some middle managers were quite hostile, saying, "If you have time to worry about this, you must not be doing your job."

All through these difficult times, two executives kept encouraging us:

> "Keep pushing! This is important. We will find the money; we will figure out the organizational issues. Go for it. Don't get discouraged."

These executive sponsors opened doors and provided the advice that ultimately got IBM into the speech recognition business. Without their encouragement, we would never have been successful.

Raising money for a new product or business is stressful. Know your friends, and when times get dark, rely on them. Nowhere is it written that you have to fight the world alone.

(P.S. If absolutely no one thinks your idea is good, perhaps you *should* have second thoughts.)

■ ■ ■

THE SAND HILL VENTURE NEWS

Clark covered the technology beat for a large Bay Area newspaper. While he loved his work, the pay was low and he could not afford to buy a house for his family. An independently wealthy friend approached him about starting a weekly newspaper reporting on the Valley's hot deals and technologies.

The idea intrigued Clark and he began writing a business plan for the *The Sand Hill Venture News.* After several weeks, he was so excited he mentioned this to his good friend and trusted colleague—the city desk editor.

The next morning Clark was fired. Ten days later, when he was allowed to collect his personal effects from his desk, his 1,500 business cards were missing. His old employer "lost" his last paycheck and Clark had to hire an attorney to get paid.

Clark freelanced until he could start his new paper. Now eight months old, *The Sand Hill Venture News* is ahead of its business plan and has almost reached the break-even point.

If you plan to leave your current employer, do not talk about your new business with your current colleagues.

■ ■ ■

In Closing

. . .

Entrepreneurs should surround themselves
with people who tell the truth.

—John Montgomery, partner,
General Counsel Associates, LLP

. . .

Starting a new business or building a new product inevitably requires you and your colleagues to learn new things and change your assumptions about the world. Developing a business plan is a blueprint for action. Whenever you advocate change, you will meet resistance. Your family, friends, and colleagues may all express their skepticism about your plans.

Ideas with the greatest profit potential are often the boldest. The bolder the plan, the more support you will need from others. Unfortunately, the bolder the idea, the more it will challenge deeply held beliefs. The most exceptional ideas are often the most controversial. The bolder the plan, the more likely people will ridicule it.

A natural reaction to your friends' and colleagues' skepticism is to get angry or depressed and stop communicating. If you keep your project secret from everyone, you may reason, then no one will criticize you. However, a strategy of secrecy usually fails, since it generates no market feedback and prevents ideas from maturing.

Secrecy may indeed protect you from criticism, but it also prevents people from supporting you. Too much introspection precludes action. Only through effective communication can you find the allies required to implement your ideas. Only through communication can you take your idea and make it a shared vision with passionate supporters.

Communicating your ideas without damaging your career can be difficult—and at times dangerous. As mentioned in the last chapter, companies sometimes fire people for expressing an interest in starting their own business. The balance between open communication and too much secrecy can be difficult.

With whom should you talk? The ultimate owner of the product usually determines this. When your current employer will own the business, your ideas are company confidential. Discuss them inside the company. Conversely, if you are building a separate business, consult with your friends and family. Avoid your current colleagues no matter how well you know them.

Over the years I have found it helpful to develop a list of people when I wish to "shop" a new idea. I write down the names and track my progress, usually talking with one or two each week. Typically a cross section of people is best. For example, you might talk with individuals from the following divisions and professions:

New Product or Service <u>Inside</u> Your Company

- Research
- Development
- Marketing
- Sales
- Corporate Office
- Other Divisions
- Classmates from Company Training Classes

New Business <u>Separate</u> from Your Existing Company

- Family
- College Friends
- Realtor
- Lawyer
- Friends of the Family
- Parents of Your Children's Classmates
- Business Associates of Your Parents

As you talk with people, listen carefully, and remember that you are doing market research. Sometimes innovative marketing and technical ideas come from unlikely sources. Explaining a project to your grandmother may prepare you for press interviews. Talking with friends may reveal unexpected sources of funding.

Whatever your idea, bear in mind that creation is one of the most rewarding human activities. It is also among the most difficult.

Best of luck. Remember to enjoy the journey, not just the destination.

APPENDICES

■ ■ ■

■ ■ ■

THE 10-SECOND PROPOSAL

The 10-second proposal is the primary method of presenting an idea via e-mail or voicemail.

After you have thought out the idea for your business or product, finding a sponsor with money is usually the next step. Ideally you would present in person, first testing the water with the three-sentence proposal described on page 105 and then followed by a business strategy presentation described on page 122. These face-to-face meetings are more effective than using e-mail or voicemail. Unfortunately, sometimes it is not possible to present in person because:

- You are too far away.
- You cannot get an appointment.
- You are not sure who is the correct executive or venture capitalist.
- There are multiple possible funding sources and you do not know who is really interested.

When it is not possible to present your idea in person, a short e-mail or voicemail is often more effective than faxes, formal letters, or long business plans. A brief e-mail or voicemail minimizes your investment, forces you to be concise, and protects you from needlessly developing a detailed written plan.

Brevity and clarity are key to pitching a new idea via e-mail or voicemail. A typical executive spends less than ten seconds reading an e-mail note, and discards many notes in less than three seconds.[45] Some executives read only the first screen of an e-mail or listen to just the first few seconds of a voicemail. Your proposal must therefore be short and engaging.

■ ■ ■

**Many people can present smoke,
but are unable to find the factual information
that investors need to understand.**

—ROY L. ROGERS,
Rogers Investment Corp.

■ ■ ■

THE E-MAIL PROPOSAL

Typically, an e-mail proposal should include:

- A dramatic subject line
- Who you are
- Why you are writing
- What your idea is
- Why your idea is good
- Your e-mail address and phone number

For example:

To: George_Brown@bigvcfirm.com

Subject: A SHAPELY GERIATRIC TOOTHBRUSH?

George,

I am Walter Smith, a student at Berkeley. Professor Kirkenbaum recommended I talk with you about a revolutionary new shape for a geriatric toothbrush. Are you funding ventures in this area? I have some preliminary drawings.

The aging population will expand the market for easy-to-hold toothbrushes.

Please let me know if you are interested or if you can recommend another source of funding.

Walter Smith
Chemical Engineering
University of California, Berkeley
wasmith@university.com
800-555-1234

Walter did not give his idea away. He told just enough to elicit a response and set up a meeting. He did not explain that he is using a new technique of injection molding. Correctly, he did reference one of his professors. Professor Kirkenbaum may know little about geriatrics or plastics; but even if he is in the English department, Walter was smart to reference him. Referencing a mutual acquaintance is generally effective (see page 112 for ideas on how to find references).

THE VOICEMAIL PROPOSAL

Typically, a voicemail proposal should include:

- Who you are
- Why you are calling
- Your idea
- Why it is a good idea
- How to reach you
- When you will call back

For example:

> "George, this is Wally Jones. I'm a getting my Ph.D. at Stanford and have been thinking about a revolutionary new nail polish. Are you interested? I've done some preliminary market research that is interesting.
> "You can reach me at 650-555-2222 or I'll call back on Friday. If you are not interested, I'd appreciate any recommendations you might have."

Notice that our aspiring entrepreneur does not explain his idea—which is a nail polish that changes colors. He gives no actual details on what the product in fact is or how it works. His objective is to find someone who has the money, is interested in his product, and is willing to talk with him in person.

THE PRODUCT CONCEPT DOCUMENT

Most high-tech companies develop new products without much documentation. Analogous to building a house without blueprints, the results are similar: poor design, unnecessary costs, and lots of overtime. Rip out a wall in a house built without blueprints, and you will find a morass of wiring and plumbing. Likewise, look under the covers of a product built without documentation and you will find an amateurish design.

As companies mature and expand, they usually stop writing business plans. Frequently they fail to replace the business plan with a new document, so they end up developing new products with no written plans. Breaking ground on a new product with no documentation first confuses engineering, then marketing, and ultimately the customer.[46]

The product concept document fixes this problem. It defines a product's objectives before engineering starts to build it. From one to three pages long, it creates a shared vision, a definition of success. It helps engineering design the product; it helps marketing craft successful programs; and it helps management know when a product is complete.

Written before the project starts, the product concept document defines the finish line. Ideally the project's sponsor—a researcher, engineer, or manager—creates the document before spending any money.

A product concept document should be short and simple. It can be an uncomplicated fill-in-the-blanks, handwritten document. Keep it simple, but enforce the discipline of writing down your goals before you spend money.[47] A typical product concept document will look something like the example below.

A Sample Product Concept Document

Description of the Product	Page 8
The Product's Objectives	Page 48
The Product's Key Features	Page 55
1.	
2.	
3.	
4.	
A Diagram or Sketch of the Product	Page 50
The Target User	Pages 10 and 64
Key Competitors	Page 38
1.	
2.	
3.	
The Target Price	Page 18
Key Milestones	Page 52

The Business Strategy Presentation

■ ■ ■

**During a presentation you are trying to convince
very intelligent people to part with
large amounts of money. If you don't believe it
yourself, you won't be able to sell it to anyone.**

—John Montgomery, partner,
General Counsel Associates, LLP

■ ■ ■

A stand-up presentation is usually more effective than
submitting a written report. Before you spend weeks or
months drafting a project plan or business plan, develop a
presentation.

A presentation will crystallize your thinking and build
support for your idea. Start by developing an outline similar to this one. If you have a team, assign each slide to an
individual.

1 **Project Name**
Date
Your Name

2 **Agenda**	
a) Summary	b) Opportunity
c) Product	d) Competition
e) Financials	f) Action Plan

3

Executive Summary

- The Customer
- The Product or Business

    (see pages 8 and 10)

4

Business Objective

- Goal
- Time Frame

    (see page 74)

5

The Opportunity

- Market Size
- Market Growth

    (see pages 26–32)

6

Demographics

    (see page 23)

7

Target Market

- The Customer
- Customer's Prequisites

    (see pages 10 and 64)

8

The Product

- What It Does
- How It Works

    (see page 8)

9

Product Schematic

- Diagram or Picture

    (see page 50)

10

Product's Benefits

- Benefits
- Unique Features

    (see page 48)

11

The Competition

- Who Are They?
- What Are They Doing?

    (see pages 37–40)

12

Competitors' Products

- Key Features
- Their Value Proposition

    (see page 42)

13

Competitive Feature Matrix

- You versus the Competition

    (see page 54)

14

Marketing Plan

- Marketing Objective
- Marketing Programs

    (see pages 76 and 84)

15 **Channel Strategy**	16 **Development Schedule**

• Distribution
• Technical Support
    (see page 79)
	• Key Milestones
	• Ship Date
	    (see page 52)

17 **Cost of Goods**	18 **Pricing**

• Competitor's Costs
• Your Costs
    (see pages 16 and 54)
	• Competitor's Pricing
	• Your Pricing
	    (see pages 18, 42, and 70)

19 **Demonstrations**	20 **Financials**

• Yours or Competitor's
• Videotapes or Samples
    (see page 56)
	• Break-even Analysis
	• Cash Requirements
	    (see page 20)

21 **Next Steps**	22 **Summary**

• What You Want from This
  Audience
	• Benefits of This Proposal
	• Actions Required
	    (see pages 106–107)

After you have developed a draft of your presentation, rehearse it. Your presentation style may be more important than the content. Rehearse the presentation in front of an audience, mirror, or video camera—something that will give you feedback. Time your presentation to make sure it is not too long.

Avoid the following common pitfalls:

Presenting with your back to the audience. Many presenters need to see their own slides as they present them, so they turn their back to the audience and read their presentation. This is completely ineffective. Several techniques can help you avoid this. Instead of turning around, glance down at the transparency on the overhead projector. Looking at the overhead projector instead of the screen will keep you facing the audience.

If your notebook PC is connected to a projector, position the notebook's screen between you and your audience. This works as a teleprompter and enables you to present facing your audience.

Avoiding eye contact with the decision maker. It is difficult to look the key decision maker in the eye while you are trying to remember your speaking points. Therefore, many presenters look at someone else. This is ineffective. Identify the decision maker. If you present in their conference room, find out where they normally sit. If it is your conference room, assign them a seat. Position yourself with your notes, the overhead projector, or the PC between you and the executive. As you are looking at your presentation, it will appear that you are looking at the executive.

Running out of time. Presentations inevitably start late. Ask the decision maker how much time he or she has. If it is less than 20 minutes, consider abandoning the presentation. Sit across the table, and present your idea in 2–3 minutes. Then stop and ask for questions.

Decision maker "no-shows." The entourage might say, "Just start and Mr. Big will join us later." Ask how long he or she will be, and if it will be less than 10 minutes, start with introductions and ask questions. In other words, stall. But at some point, you will have to start. If you do not know what the decision maker looks like, assign someone the introduction task. For example, you might say, "When your senior partner arrives, would you stop me and introduce us?"

When the decision maker finally arrives, stop, summarize what you have presented, and ask whether he or she has questions.

Unknown audience. You are ushered into a conference room and have no idea who the decision maker is. Ask the group, "Could someone do introductions?" If introductions omit titles, interrupt and ask them all to describe their job responsibilities.

THE WRITTEN BUSINESS PLAN

■ ■ ■

Silicon Valley moves very quickly;
people don't spend much time looking at
business plans. They look at the executive
summary, the financials, and the biographies.

—JOHN MONTGOMERY, PARTNER,
General Counsel Associates, LLP

■ ■ ■

If you have neither a source of funding nor an executive
sponsor, proceed cautiously. A lengthy business plan may
not solve your funding problems. You should find one or
more co-sponsors before you invest months writing a detailed plan. If you have been unable to build enthusiasm
for your idea verbally, you are unlikely to sell it in writing.
Normally you should be able to obtain some level of commitment from a presentation (see page 101) before you
would write an extensive plan.

Cautions aside, a detailed business plan can serve several critical functions. For example, it can solidify bank
and venture capital funding, and it can sell a large organization on funding a new product line or a new division.[48]

Writing a business plan involves more than processing
words. You must develop a clear vision and sell it to your
target reader. The following steps are helpful:

1. Make sure you know why you are writing a business plan.

2. Identify your target audience.

3. Get samples of business plans that your target audience likes. Usually you should ask the readers themselves for samples they personally prefer.

4. Interview others who have written successful business plans for this audience. Get copies of their plans and interview them to learn about the steps they went through. Pay particular attention to whom they presented and in what order. Ask who their inside salesperson was.

5. Develop an outline for your business plan.

6. Write the parts you know first and circulate your partial plan as a draft.

Remember, a business plan alone will not secure funding. You may still have to develop a presentation (see page 122) to complement your business plan.

■ ■ ■

**Every venture capitalist I talked to asked for a
business plan, and I just said "no." Instead,
I chalk-talked them through our plans on their
whiteboard. We obtained more financing than
we needed.**

—DALE L. FULLER, PRESIDENT AND CEO,
WhoWhere? Inc.

■ ■ ■

THE BUSINESS PLAN OUTLINE

■ ■ ■

The number one problem with most business plans
is the executive summary. Simple, easy-to-
understand executive summaries are tough to write.

—ROY L. ROGERS,
Rogers Investment Corp.

■ ■ ■

The following illustrates the framework of a typical business plan.

Cover Sheet	Name of the business and the authors
Executive Summary	Pages 8 and 74
Industry Overview	Pages 23 to 34
Description of Product or Business	Pages 8 and 48
Diagrams or Pictures of the Product	Page 50
Target Customer	Pages 10 and 61–68
Competition	Pages 37–44 and 54
Marketing, Sales, and Distribution	Pages 72–86
Pricing	Pages 18, 42, and 70
Schedules	Page 52
Management	Managers' Biographies
Financials[49]	Page 20
Supporting Documentation	Analyst's Reports

THE PRODUCT DEVELOPMENT SCORECARD

The product development scorecard predicts the likelihood that you will produce a great product. Over time you should adjust this checklist to reflect the actual history of your products.

If you are part of an ongoing enterprise, develop a scorecard that, in hindsight, would have predicted your successes and failures. This is likely to be a good predictor of future successes and failures. If you manage multiple projects, require each project manager to present this checklist at your quarterly reviews before you authorize additional funding.

Score each question as follows:

No, and not planned	=	0
No, but planned	=	4
50% true	=	5
80% true	=	8
Yes, definitely true	=	10
	(maximum of points 10 per question)	

If a document exists and is out of date, kept secret, or ignored, do not give yourself more than four points. A ten is for accurate, widely read, and appropriately used documentation. You may give yourself negative points, for example, if you are developing for an outdated operating environment.

Will Your Development Team Produce a Great Product?

Score

☐ **One Sentence Product Definition**
Can development describe the product in simple-to-understand terms (see page 8)?

☐ **Target User**
Can development describe the target user? (see page 10)

☐ **Prerequisites and Environment**
Are the prerequisites and customer's operating environment documented? (see page 64)

☐ **Design Objectives**
Are the design objectives simply documented on one sheet of paper? (see pages 43 and 48)

☐ **Drawings and Pictures**
Is there a sketch of what the product will look like and a diagram of how it will work? (see page 50)

☐ **Competitive Knowledge**
Are the competitors' features documented side-by-side with yours? (see page 55)

☐ **Engineering Experience**
Do your developers use your product and your competitors' products daily? (see page 97)

☐ **Published Schedule**
Is there a one-page schedule tracking three to ten key dates? (see page 52)

☐ **Realistic Cost Targets**
Will the product's development and manufacturing costs create an affordable product? (see pages 16 and 18)

☐ **Rapid Prototyping Capability**
Will you use an iterative design technique? (see page 56)

☐ **Marketing And Development Agreement**
Have research, development, and marketing agreed on the project's objectives? (see page 43)

☐ **TOTAL**

Scoring

Over 100 Too good to be true
90–100 A winner in the making
80–89 Good start
Under 80 Still needs work; high risk if you are within three months of launch

The Marketing, Sales, and Distribution Scorecard

Developing a marketing, sales, and distribution scorecard enables you to track the progress of activities outside R&D. Over time you should adjust this checklist, as you would the Product Development Scorecard, to reflect the actual history of your products or business.

Again, if you are part of an ongoing enterprise, develop a scorecard that, in hindsight, would have predicted your successes and failures. Such a rating system is likely to be a good predictor of future success or failure. If you manage multiple projects, require each project manager to present this checklist at the quarterly reviews before you authorize additional funding.

Score each question as follows:

No, and not planned	= 0
No, but planned	= 4
Partially complete	= 6
Yes, with reservations	= 6
Not applicable	= 8
Yes, definitely	= 10
(Maximum of points 10 per question)	

Will Your Marketing Plan Succeed?

Score

☐ **Target Customer Identified**
Can you describe the buyer of your product? (see pages 10 and 64)

☐ **Customer Demographics**
Do you know your customers' ages, income levels, and such? (see pages 23 and 67)

☐ **Customers Interviewed**
Have you interviewed ten potential customers? (One point per customer) (see page 62 and 63)

☐ **Committed Customers**
Have ten customers agreed to buy specific volumes at an agreed-upon price? (see page 70)

☐ **Retail Visits**
Have you visited ten retail outlets and interviewed the store managers? (see page 12)

☐ **Sales Estimates**
Have ten sales managers or store managers given you sales estimates that support your revenue plan? (also page 12)

☐ **Product Focus Groups**
Have you shown your product to potential customers? (see page 68)

☐ **Field Testing**
Have customers used the product or prototype and given positive feedback? (see page 22)

☐ **Marketing Focus Groups**
Have you tested your packaging, marketing materials, and advertising programs? (see page 59)

☐ **Written Marketing Plan**
Do you have a written marketing plan? (see page 84)

☐ **Distributors Interviewed**
Have you interviewed two distributors in each of your largest markets? (see page 12)

☐ **Distributors Committed**
Have you signed a distribution agreement in each of
your target markets? (also page 12)

☐ **Diagram of Your Distribution and Support Plan**
Have you developed a diagram of your distribution and
technical support plan? (see page 78)

☐ **TOTAL**

Scoring

Over 100 Too good to be true
90–100 A winner in the making
80–89 Good start
Under 80 Still needs work; high risk if you are within 30 days of
launch

ANSWERS TO GREY POUPON VALUE PROPOSITION QUIZ

Please fill in the form on page 42 before you read this.

Since a product identical to Grey Poupon sells for $1.39, this amount represents the price of basic Dijon mustard. Because specialty mustard is one of life's small pleasures, the $1.39 customers pay for it is allocated to enjoying life or improving comfort. What justifies the 80¢ premium for Grey Poupon Dijon mustard? Is it the name? Is it the attractive bottle?

If the buyer does not trust store brands, the remaining 80¢ goes to lowering risk. However, if the buyer trusts the store brand and has had good success with their products, why is he or she paying an additional 80¢? Possibly because it maintains status and avoids embarrassment with the neighbors. Who wants to put a store brand in front of guests?

Grey Poupon is a status mustard. In fact, Nabisco's TV ads for Grey Poupon feature two Rolls Royces. The message is clear: Successful people use Grey Poupon.

GREY POUPON'S VALUE PROPOSITION

☐ Save Time	$_____	☑ Lower Risk	$ .40
☐ Save Money	$_____	☑ Maintain Status	$ .40
☐ Make Money	$_____	☑ Enjoy Life	$ 1.39
		☐ Improve Comfort	$_____
		☐ Survive (a necessity)	$_____
		☐ _____ Other	$_____

ANATOMY OF A PRESS RELEASE

■ ■ ■

Financial markets respond to good PR.

—SCOTT A. RYLES, MANAGING DIRECTOR AND HEAD
OF GLOBAL TECHNOLOGY INVESTMENT BANKING,
Merrill Lynch

■ ■ ■

Primary Headline

The headline should capture the essence of the release and encourage further reading. Many editors only read the headlines, so make them exciting! Include keywords, such as "kitchen" and "cooking," because some publications search for specific topics.

Subhead

Opening

The first paragraph must be short and include a story angle. Here the story angle is, "the world's first."

FOR IMMEDIATE RELEASE:

**L'CHEF REVOLUTIONIZES
FRENCH COOKING**

**WORLD'S FIRST TALKING
KITCHEN ASSISTANT**

LAS VEGAS, Nev.—Palo Alto Boheme, Inc., today unveiled L'Chef, the world's first talking kitchen assistant. Retailing for under $200, L'Chef talks the aspiring home chef through the subtleties of French cooking.

First Two Paragraphs

The opening paragraphs should tell the story and spark the reader's curiosity. The more provocative the opening paragraphs, the more likely the story will be picked up by the media.

Technical Details

Include a few technical details early in the release. On the second page, include one to four paragraphs of features. Describe how it works, and what the benefits are to the user.

L'Chef resembles a mouse and uses a patented wireless technology to communicate between the kitchen and a home PC. The mouse's tail is actually an antenna.

After selecting a recipe on a PC, L'Chef talks the home cook through the recipe. Stylishly engineered, L'Chef's five buttons—Pause, Help, Back-up, Skip, and Start Again—enable both novice and expert to produce extraordinary cuisine.

"The microprocessor will revolutionize the kitchen," said world-renowned French chef turned innovator, Pierre d'Coutre, who demonstrated L'Chef at the Consumer Electronics Show in Las Vegas (booth 21055).

Strong Quote

Profound, somewhat controversial, the quotation should frame the product in a larger story. The person quoted should have time to do media interviews. If he or she does not, use a second quotation from the VP of Marketing.

Inventor's Bio

The human side of the story often gets significant media attention. Include it in the press release.

D'Coutre is the owner and head chef of the Palo Alto Boheme Restaurant. Previously d'Coutre taught at. . . .

Press Contact

The press contact should check his or her voicemail frequently and have direct access to the executive quoted in the release.

Press Contact: Sue Smith, phone number, e-mail address

Sales Information: Joe Sales Manager, phone number

Web site: www.l'chef.com

Sales Contact

If this is an 800 number or receptionist, make sure the person answering the phone knows about the release.

Prepare an information package that can be mailed or faxed to callers.

Web Site

Include your Web site if it has current information on the product. The Web site should have the press release, background on the company and its executives, technical details, prices, and pictures.

TRADE SHOWS

Trade shows can be an invaluable tool in finding distributors and corporate customers. They can also be an unproductive distraction. Here are some tips on how to use trade shows early in the product development cycle when you are looking for financing, strategic partnerships, master distributors, or that one big order. To get the most from your participation in a trade show:

Make appointments. Make a list of people who might resell your product. Call them or hire someone to call them. Over the years I have had success hiring hourly contractors (usually recent college graduates) to find, call, and schedule appointments with potential partners.

Visit retailers, VARs, distributors, and OEMs. Identify someone who looks competent in their booth. Introduce yourself. Get a business card and state your purpose clearly: "I'm looking for a distributor for a _____ product; may I speak with someone here about that?" If no one is available, get the name and number of the VP of Marketing or Business Development.

Advertise for channel partners. If you have a booth or pedestal at the show, display a sign saying, "Distributor Inquiries Welcomed" or "New York Distributor Needed." If you need foreign distributors, use multilingual signs.

Most industries have several domestic and international trade shows. Select the right ones. Look for shows that will help you meet your current business objectives. New businesses often need more dealers or more corporate customers.

The following list describes the largest and best-known trade shows for high-tech consumer products. Attending them will help keep your pulse on the industry. They are a great place to watch your competitors, but they are so large and expensive that small companies can become lost.

CeBIT Europe's largest computer trade show. Spread across several exposition halls on the Hanover fairgrounds, CeBIT attracts over 750,000 people each year in March. This German trade show attracts manufacturers from around the world announcing products for the European market.

CES The Winter Consumer Electronics Show is North America's major trade show for announcing consumer products. Winter CES is always in Las Vegas in early January. Summer CES is often combined with other trade shows.

COMDEX Fall COMDEX is North America's largest personal computer trade show. Held each year in November, it brings 200,000 people to Las Vegas. Many new products and companies debut at this show. There is also a smaller Spring COMDEX and several international expositions, including one in Beijing.

E3 The Electronic Entertainment Expo is probably America's noisiest high-tech trade show. Usually held in the spring, game and educational software companies hype their products for the Christmas season.

ANSWERS TO MARKETING SAVVY QUIZ

Please take the quiz on page 77 before you read these answers.

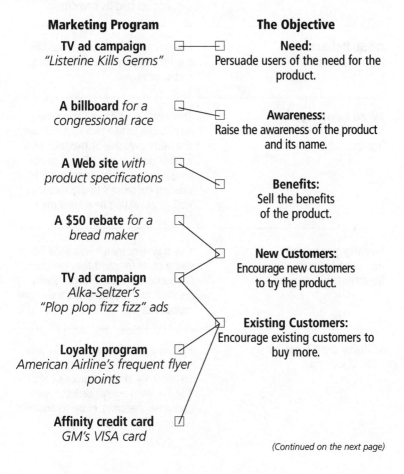

Marketing Program		The Objective
TV ad campaign *"Listerine Kills Germs"*		**Need:** Persuade users of the need for the product.
A billboard *for a congressional race*		**Awareness:** Raise the awareness of the product and its name.
A Web site *with product specifications*		**Benefits:** Sell the benefits of the product.
A $50 rebate *for a bread maker*		
TV ad campaign *Alka-Seltzer's "Plop plop fizz fizz" ads*		**New Customers:** Encourage new customers to try the product.
Loyalty program *American Airline's frequent flyer points*		**Existing Customers:** Encourage existing customers to buy more.
Affinity credit card *GM's VISA card*		

(Continued on the next page)

TV ad campaign: "Listerine Kills Germs"	When these TV ads originally aired, few consumers knew they needed a mouthwash that killed germs, thus these ads developed the need for a germ-killing mouthwash.
A billboard for a congressional race	Political billboards usually have little content but do increase name recognition.
A Web site with product specifications	Consumers visit a product's Web site in search of more information about the product and its benefits.
A $50 Rebate for a bread maker	Few households use two bread makers. This large rebate attracts new, first-time buyers.
TV ad campaign: Alka-Seltzer's "Plop plop fizz fizz" ads	This vintage ad campaign encouraged users to use two Alka-Seltzers. The label says one or two, but who would use only one? Plop-fizz no longer sounds right. It encouraged existing customers to use more, as well as attracting new customers.
Loyalty program: American Airline's frequent flyer program	Few travelers try a new airline because of its frequent flyer program. Domestic frequent flyer programs create brand loyalty and encourage repeat usage.
Affinity credit cards: GM's VISA card	Primarily used by existing GM owners; every credit card purchase lowers the cost of a consumer's next GM car. With every purchase, the consumer becomes more committed to buying GM again.

ADDITIONAL READING

Business books which are both useful and interesting to read are rare. A small number stand out. Here are my favorites; I hope you enjoy them:

The Twenty-Two Immutable Laws of Marketing, by Al Ries and Jack Trout.

Ries and Trout have extraordinary insights into business strategy, planning, and product management. This is arguably the best business strategy book in existence. A few of the "laws" may not apply to all businesses. This is a must-read book for all business executives.

Guerrilla Marketing, by Jay Conrad Levinson.

Guerrilla Marketing contains hundreds of inexpensive ways to stretch a limited marketing budget. Whether you are rich or poor, if you are developing a marketing program, Levinson will help you stretch your dollars.

Guerrilla Marketing has so many great ideas, it can be overwhelming. An inexperienced marketer might try to implement every suggestion in the book. Instead, use *Guerrilla Marketing* like a cookbook, trying one or two new recipes each month and then reusing your favorites. An interactive CD version is also available.

For small businesses, guerrilla marketing is usually more effective than a large advertising budget. Large advertising budgets may force small businesses into bankruptcy. *Guerrilla Marketing* enables a new business to try various approaches while conserving cash.

Starting on a Shoestring: Building a Business Without a Bankroll, by Arnold
    S. Goldstein, Ph.D.

Starting on a Shoestring is an excellent book for individuals
starting their first business and for general managers of any
business concerned about conserving cash. Goldstein contin-
uously challenges the reader to spend less without sacrificing
results. Many high-tech start-ups would benefit from his
pragmatic suggestions. Anyone investing their own money in
a business should read this book cover to cover. Goldstein is
readable, yet thorough, covering many topics aspiring entrepreneurs usually miss.

*The World Is Your Market: How to Profit from the Vast Opportunities Outside
    Our Border,* by John Newlin.

This is an enjoyable-to-read, factual book on international
business that should be in every executive's library. Newlin
has a subtle sense of humor and a pragmatic style that packs
a lot of information into a pleasant read.

Leadership Secrets of Attila the Hun, by Wess Roberts.

Wess Roberts emphasizes deference to leadership and loyalty
as key elements of success in middle management. If you
have trouble selling your insights to the tribal leadership of
your company, this book may help.

This is also an excellent book for young managers who
have not yet learned the importance of making the tribal
chief (their boss) look good.

Churchill on Leadership—Executive Success in the Face of Adversity, by
    Steven F. Hayward.

Set against the backdrop of two world wars, *Churchill on Leadership* emphasizes the uncertainty and complexity of executive
decisions. It cautions against relying on numbers when experience is a better guide. It leaves the reader with the impres-
sion that great leadership is hard work, which it is.

Young MBAs should read this book cautiously. Emulating Churchill's management style early in a career is unlikely to result in a satisfactory outcome—for the aspiring leader or their colleagues.

Shogun, by James Clavell.

Shogun is a great novel with many insights into executive leadership. An epic tale, told by one of great novelists of our time, it is set in Japan during its early contacts with Western society.

Clavell's portrait of samurai leadership, its attention to detail, and its thorough questioning of subordinates has shaped my management style. Naturally, some of the samurai warrior's management techniques are not appropriate in the modern workplace.

Karen's Kittycat Club, by Ann M. Martin. Part of *The Babysitter's Little Sister* Series, Volume 4.

A children's book, this is the story of a cat-sitting service founded by three seven-year-olds. It chronicles many of the problems encountered by start-ups:

- Squabbles between the founders
- Unrealistic market sizing
- Credibility problems with customers
- Second guessing the product definition

Each chapter is food for an evening's discussion with your children, spouse, or colleagues.

NOTES

INTRODUCTION: GLOBAL LEADERSHIP

1. Price Waterhouse National Venture Capital Survey and the San Jose Office of Economic Development.

2. Silicon Valley's largest city, San Jose, is 51% Hispanic and Asian/Pacific Islander. San Jose has one of the highest levels of workforce education in the U.S. and *the lowest* crime rate of any American city with a population over 250,000. The low crime rate is indicative of the racial harmony in the valley.

3. Valley cities also have a reputation for clean government with little patronage. Bribes and professional "expediters"—common in other parts of the world—are rare in Silicon Valley. The lesson is clear: Local governments will attract business investment if they are:
- Business friendly
- Predictable
- Devoid of corruption
- Quick to approve or disapprove new construction

4. Many first-time product managers erroneously assume that engineers will have little interest in a product's financial and marketing plans. Most engineers have a deep interest in the business model and the marketing plans surrounding their products. If you post or publish engineering's scores and targets, make sure you post a similar marketing report card. It may be helpful to have everyone involved read *The Silicon Valley Way* and agree on which techniques are relevant to your business.

CHAPTER 2: SEVEN QUESTIONS EXECUTIVES ASK

5. Who Will Sell It? (page 12)

Finding an effective sales channel is often more difficult than designing a product. The personal computer game software industry exemplifies this problem. According to the *Wall Street Journal* (June 19, 1997), 4,000 software game titles are available. The average software store carries 50, about 1% of the available titles.

Imagine developing a product that only 1% of the retail stories are likely to stock. This problem is not unique to software. Whether you are making cosmetics or gaskets, finding an effective sales channel will be key to your success. A distributor alone is rarely sufficient. Most of these 4,000 software titles have a distributor but are still not available in retail stores.

Two sections later in the book—"How Will You Sell and Support the Product?" on page 78 and "Who Will Generate Demand?" on page 80— can help you develop an effective sales channel.

6. How Many People Will Buy It? (page 14)

One-tenth of one percent is inevitably wrong. Finding the correct percentage is challenging. You may be able to capture a higher percentage of a market if you have a clearly defined target market or a weak competitor. Pages 15 and 33 outline more precise, but more time-consuming, technique for estimating sales.

Before you invest money you should validate your sales estimate by:

- Finding others who have already done what you want to do. Ask them what their sales were. If you want to start an air charter service, talk with air charter businesses in other parts of the country.
- Developing a sales estimate as a percentage of your competitor's revenue. How many units do your competitors sell? What percentage of their business can you capture?

Both of these techniques use other existing businesses—not market size—to develop sales estimates. I usually do both—developing a sales estimate from market data and from competitive data.

7. How Much Will It Cost? (page 16)

Different companies and different executives use the word "cost" to mean three decidedly different things. In the software example on page 16, cost refers to the total cash a project will need during the year, as in, "What is the annual cost of the project?" In this example, the answer would be, "About $8 million a year." Some business school professors cringe at this use of the word "cost," but to the executive, the project is "costing" $8 million.

A second and very common use of the word "cost" means retail price, as in "How much does a Big Mac cost?" I cringe at *this* use because it confuses cost with retail price.

The correct, but least frequently used, meaning of cost is the *cost of manufacture* or the *cost of providing the service,* as in the espresso machine example on page 17.

Different industries and executives favor different meanings of cost. Software executives rarely worry about the cost of manufacture; instead, they worry about the cost of development. Plant managers use cost to mean the cost of manufacture or the cost of parts.

It is wise to know the whole cost equation for your product, so that you can answer any question. When selling a new project, think through which piece of the cost equation you should present first. A $14 cost of parts sounds better than $8 million of development.

8. It is unbelievable but true—sales, marketing, and general and administrative costs are three times as expensive as R&D in a typical software company. On average R&D is less than 20% of a software company's total costs (*Soft Letter, Trends and Strategies in Software Publishing,* February 28, 1997, 617-924-3944).

9. Silicon Deli's Espresso Machine (page 17)

Andy pays his people about $7/hour (plus benefits). How does his marginal cost of labor jump to $28? Andy's employees are unwilling to work less than four hours in the middle of the day. Most workers will not to go to work for one hour, earn $7, and then go home. So Andy's shortest daytime shift is four hours, or $28. Andy does 50% of his business between noon and 1:00. He is very busy for one hour. He has more help than he needs before noon and after 1:00, but not enough during lunch. If Andy hires an extra person, he will pay for four hours and only get one hour of incremental revenue. Andy's marginal cost of labor during lunch is actually higher when he includes benefits.

Many high-tech businesses have marginal costs that fall rapidly. Semiconductors manufactured in small volumes are expensive, but costs usually drop quickly as volumes increase.

The difference between average cost and marginal (or incremental) cost is difficult to visualize and troublesome to many professionals. But if you do not understand how much it costs you to produce one incremental unit of production, you will price large orders poorly and may develop business plans that erode margins.

10. When Will You Break Even? (page 20)

"Accounting techniques and earnings are less important than cashflow in determining a company's value. The key to success is to maximize the realization of cashflow." William M. Cockrum, Professor, Anderson School of Management at UCLA.

If you are starting your own business and need help with the financials, see the worksheets and excellent commentary in chapter 13 of *The Successful Business Plan: Secrets and Strategies* by Rhonda M. Abrams.

If you are preparing financials for a venture capitalist or investment banker, ask them for copies of previous successful proposals and hire an accountant.

In the early years of a business, cash flow may be more important than profit. Run out of cash and you can go out of business. However, calculating and projecting cash flow correctly is difficult and time-consuming, so most executives initially construct a simple P&L (or income statement) similar to the one shown on page 20.

While most executives weigh the initial merits of a project with a back-of-a-napkin P&L, before they commit funds they will scrutinize the following:

1. Balance Sheet
2. Monthly Cash Budget
3. Income Statement (P&L)
4. Statement of Cash Flows

These documents are critical for mergers, acquisitions, and investments consuming more than 10% of your net worth. Most banks will also require them for bank loans.

11. The bottom line of this short income statement labeled *Profit (or Loss)* is the Operating Income, also called Earnings Before Interest and Taxes "EBIT."

12. The Silicon Insider's Cash Flow Problem (page 21)

Dave's cash flow problems killed him during an economic downturn, but many small businesses also have cash flow problems during the good times.

Small and medium-size manufacturing companies often pay cash on delivery for their supplies, but their customers may take 45 to 60 days to pay for finished goods. If a business is successful and expands rapidly, it will require ever more cash, even if it is profitable.

Service businesses, such as temporary agencies, have an equally challenging problem. They may pay their people weeks or months before they collect from their customers. If the business expands rapidly, it will require increasing amounts of cash to meet its payroll.

Chapter 3: Market Research

13. What Do the Neighbors Think? (page 24)

The idea was to develop a 900 number with travel advice and discounts for parents and retired professionals. I had done a fair amount of market research on the size of the travel industry and how much consumers could save with better advice. Even though the market opportunity was large, no one wanted to pay for the advice given over a 900 number.

This is typical of many failed projects; the market is big, but the idea is lame. This sort of self-deception is common in market research. The demographic data is used to hide the fact that the product concept is weak or too expensive. Validating demographic data with user interviews and focus groups usually exposes products that will not sell.

14. What's on the Web? (page 28)

America Online is probably the most widely used *Internet Service Provider* or ISP. Talk with friends and neighbors to get recommendations on the fastest, most reliable service in your area.

15. Washington has had several famous politicians leave electronic audit trails that would later embarrass them. Vice President Al Gore's phone records have caused him some embarrassment. Oliver North, a national security aide to Ronald Reagan, was unaware that the White House mainframe computer was keeping copies of his e-mail, even after he erased them. Many companies keep nightly or weekly back-up tapes of their e-mail systems and can reconstruct an individual's e-mail traffic.

16. Bookmarks are defined in the glossary on page 161.

17. The Coyote Creek Gas Station (page 33)

Numbers given are estimates. Please collect your *own* data before buying a gas station or a garlic farm.

CHAPTER 4: THE COMPETITION

18. The Competition (page 37)

Al Ries and Jack Trout in *The Twenty-Two Immutable Laws of Marketing* present a persuasive argument against building incrementally better products and attacking your competitor head-on. In other words, if there are two bakeries on Main Street, you should open a bagel shop not a third bakery.

19. What Are Their Secrets? (page 44)

Ira Winkler documents a good example of help wanted ads that reveal too much in his book, *Corporate Espionage: What It Is; Why It's Happening in Your Company; What You Must Do About It.* Individuals concerned about corporate security should read this book.

20. One such search service is: Individual Inc.'s HeadsUp service at 617-273-6020.

21. Secrets of Manufacturing (page 45)

Recently an executive of a national security firm was showing me the electronics in their home security system and explaining that it was superior to that of their competitors. I must have looked skeptical because he then opened his desk drawer and placed his competitors' partially disassembled alarm system in front of me. Each part had a little sticker with its price.

CHAPTER 5: THE PRODUCT

22. What Will It Look Like? (page 50)

It is useful to produce an *annotated* copy of your sketches and diagrams. Notes like "Large, easy-to-read display" or "Guests will see the chef through this opening" convey the key features of your vision.

Well-run companies in the service sector also use this technique. Many restaurants keep a Plexiglas blueprint of their restaurants so the host can assign tables and servers.

Call centers (for 800-numbers) often keep diagrams of what questions to ask in which sequence.

A picture really is worth 1,000 words (about four pages of text). Draw or diagram your product and your business before you write about it. This will help you avoid misunderstandings and communicate your vision more clearly than pages of word-processed notes.

23. When Will It Ship? (page 52)

Keeping high-tech projects on track is tough. An excellent and sometimes humorous book on the nuts and bolts of how to manage high-tech projects is *Rapid Development: Taming Wild Software Schedules* by Steve McConnell.

24. Brand Image (page 59)

The example of Honda renaming their cars Acura, changing their image, and charging a premium comes from *The Twenty-Two Immutable Laws of Marketing* by Al Ries and Jack Trout. Ries and Trout have great insight into the subtleties of product naming and the influence that geography and history have on consumers' perceptions.

CHAPTER 6: THE CUSTOMER

25. What Are Your Customer's Secrets? (page 66)

For more information on researching customers and competitors, see pages 26, 28, and 44.

26. The Commercial Service, part of the U.S. Department of Commerce, can be invaluable in finding foreign distributors and partners.

27. Should You Do Focus Groups? (page 68)

An excellent resource for organizations considering focus groups is *The Handbook for Focus Group Research* by Thomas L. Greenbaum.

For a fascinating new twist on focus groups and consumer research, read Ronald B. Lieber's article, "Storytelling: A New Way to Get Close to Your Customer" in the February 3, 1997, issue of *Fortune* magazine. Lieber recounts how Kimberly Clark's research into consumers' feelings—shame about toilet training—led to the development of training pants. He also describes Intuit's "follow me home plan," which sends engineers to customers' homes to observe how they use Quicken.

CHAPTER 7: THE MARKETING STRATEGY

28. Test Your Marketing Savvy (page 77)

This famous TV ad featured people with indigestion and the jingle, "Plop, plop, fizz, fizz, oh what a relief it is."

29. GM's VISA card credits a percentage of every VISA purchase toward the customer's next GM car purchase.

30. Who Will Generate Demand? (page 80)

A manufacturer's representative sells or distributes a product for a percentage of revenue. They usually work for themselves, not for the manufacturer, and they often represent multiple companies. Since manufacturer's reps are not employees, they conserve cash. The downside is that the manufacturer has less control over sales.

31. Common Misconceptions (page 81)

The World Is Your Market: How to Profit from the Vast Opportunities Outside Our Border, by John Newlin, offers superb advice on how to sell overseas. Chapter 4, "How to Explore and Enter a Country" and its sub chapter, "To What Extent Do You Want to Be Involved," should help any business ease into foreign operations.

32. Will You Need Marketing or Sales? (page 82)

A VAR, or *value added reseller,* buys a product—often a PC—and "adds value" when they resell it. VARs sometimes focus on niche markets such as physician practices or restaurant systems.

33. The role of the product manager varies widely between companies. As a project grows, pieces of the product manager's job move elsewhere. Logistics becomes a dedicated job for another individual or department. A marcom—Marketing Communications—manager may assist the product manager and design the packaging as well as brochures, fact sheets, and Web site.

34. How Much Should You Spend on Marketing and Sales? (page 83)

High-tech companies struggle to decide how much to spend on marketing and advertising. This is particularly difficult for major product introductions. *The Harvard Business Review,* November–December 1995, published an excellent—and very realistic—case study entitled, "Can This High-Tech Product Sell Itself?" written by Thomas W. Virden. Virden captures the dilemma that many high-tech companies face when launching new products.

35. What Is the Marketing Plan? (page 84)

In large organizations, run several brainstorming sessions and include your sales, engineering, and research teams. To help stimulate creative ideas, give participants a copy of *Guerrilla Marketing* by Jay Conrad Levinson.

For brainstorming to work effectively, participants must agree *not* to evaluate ideas when they are proposed. List all the ideas on a whiteboard. When the group has exhausted its ideas, take a straw vote. Ask the participants to select the five ideas they think could have the most impact. This prevents one individual with strong opinions from dominating the discussion. A straw vote may also build a quick consensus, avoiding needless discussion.

36. For more information on trade shows see the appendix on pages 139–140.

37. How Do You Become Front Page News? (page 86)

It is easy to become caught up in the hype of new business, saying too much and later disappointing customers. "Untold Fortunes: How the Cocky Consumer Startups Went Bust" by Junko Yoshida in *OEM* magazine, October 1996, details the dangers of hyping your technology too soon.

In the euphoria of media attention, it is easy to unintentionally reveal too much. In *Corporate Espionage,* Ira Winkler recounts a chilling story of a visit to a biotechnology company by a Japanese TV crew, ostensibly filming a documentary.

New technology stories are so exciting that the researcher, the developer, and the executive all want to tell the story—inevitably too much of the story. To prevent yourself and your colleagues from re-vealing too many details, prepare a one-page executive summary, usu-ally in bulleted list format. This executive summary is really a list of speaking points or sound bites. It should outline the need for the tech-nology and why the problem is so difficult to solve, and should remind the interviewee not to explain the key details of how the technology works.

CHAPTER 8: CONFRONTING THE TRUTH

38. Confronting the Truth (page 89)

The product was the IBM Speech Server, a client-server, speaker-depen-dent, large-vocabulary, speech recognition system. Journalists prone to repetitive stress injuries (RSI) used it to dictate their stories.

39. AT&T and EO (page 93)

After AT&T shut down EO, I visited their deserted Silicon Valley facil-ity. It was enormous. I walked around counting desks and figured that it took over $2 million a month to run the facility and pay the salaries.

The three remaining employees were auctioning everything. The lamps, desks, executive furniture, PCs—everything, including the patents, was for sale. One room had dozens of whiteboards; another had twenty overhead projectors.

Why did a start-up need *twenty* overhead projectors? I remember thinking, "Too many presentations and not enough thought."

It was a sobering reminder of a business run amuck:
- Too ambitious
- Too many people
- Too expensive
- No clearly defined customer need
- No focus

They had flunked the most basic back-of-a-napkin analysis (see page 4).

40. IBM's Speech Team (page 97)

The product was the IBM Speech Server. It required expensive servers and hard-to-get audio cards with a custom-built DSP (Digital Signal Processor—a microprocessor customized to process acoustic signals).

Because of the expense of the necessary hardware, it was difficult to persuade finance to buy it for marketing, sales, and engineering.

The IBM Speech Server begot many children—the IBM Personal Dictation System, IBM VoiceType, and IBM ViaVoice. With each new generation, the products became cheaper and easier to use. With each new generation, more IBM engineers used the product and more people bought it.

41. Chip's Limited Partnership (page 99)

Limited partnerships have trapped many astute business people into commitments they later regretted. On the surface Chip's limited partnership—three years of flying—seems attractive. Yet, the partnership agreement puts Chip at the beck and call of six doctors, whose business and vacation needs will inevitably conflict with Chip's schooling.

Chip wanted to fly, not run a limited partnership with six doctors. Chip's passion for flying almost caused him to enter into a business arrangement with many peripheral responsibilities that Chip did not want.

The statements in Question 40: *Will I enjoy the day-to-day management of this project? Can I exit the deal easily if it does not work?* saved Chip from three years of grief.

CHAPTER 9: RAISING MONEY

42. Counterpoint (page 103)

There is a case for investing *some* of your money—but not the kids' college funds—even in high-tech start-ups. "The Next Bill Gates?" by Bronwyn Fryer in the March 1997 issue of *Working Woman* tells the story of Kim Polese, founder and CEO of Marimba. Polese left her job as a product manger at Sun to start Marimba. She and her partners—all Java experts—eschewed venture capital and each contributed $15,000 to start Marimba. After they had developed a working prototype, they accepted $4 million from Kleiner Perkins Caufield & Byers. According to *Working Woman,* Polese and her colleagues ultimately raised more money and own more of their company because of their upfront personal investment.

43. What Do You Say to the Potential Investors (page 104)

This last question, "What would cause you to change your mind?" is important for executives who are supporting you and for executives who have declined to help you. You want to know when your early support-ers will abandon you and when the skeptics will join you.

44. Can You Impress a Venture Capitalist? (page 106)

"Looking for Lasting Profits in IPOs," *Worth* magazine, September 1996.

APPENDICES

45. The 10-Second Proposal (pages 116–117)

I confess these numbers—3 to 10 seconds per e-mail note—are from my own observation, not a large-scale, scientific study. They may over-state how much time executives actually spend on a typical e-mail.

46. The Product Concept Document (page 120)

IBM is an exception that proves the rule. Through good times and bad, when I was at IBM, the company required its product planners to write business plans. If the business plan was incomplete, the product was not announced.

Paradoxically, this discipline did not extend to initiating a project. Any executive with money in his or her budget could start developing a new product. With the hurdles at the end of a project, most product planners wrote their business plans during the last 90 days of develop-ment, when the product was 80% complete.

While IBM's business plans had a strict format, the documentation used to *start* development had no set format. The requirements received by engineering at the beginning of a project were often sparse, some-times nonexistent and rarely consistent from project to project.

The propensity to start projects without a design document is not unique to IBM; it is endemic in Silicon Valley. At cocktail parties in the Valley, I frequently ask engineering and marketing managers how their companies document product requirements. Inevitably they look to the heavens and then describe a process that usually makes the Three Stooges look organized. In some companies, the press release announc-ing the product is the first attempt to document the product's objectives.

Disorganization aside, many Valley companies, like IBM, are very successful at building products with little design documentation. Companies succeed because their engineers are bright and because high-tech products are not like buildings. Successful leading-edge product design requires iteration and user feedback. So many high-tech products do not need precise design documents on the first day of the project.

Nevertheless, a product needs an objective. When a business plan or marketing requirement's document is not available at the start of a project, a short product concept document will help focus an engineering team. If engineering must build a house without blueprints, it is helpful to provide a rough sketch. This rough sketch is the product concept document.

47. In many companies, the first document produced for a new product is the "requirements document" or the "marketing requirements document," often called the "MRD." An MRD typically has all the features of a short business plan (see page 129). Because the MRD is thorough, engineering usually starts before it is written. And therein lies the great weakness of most MRDs: they fail to provide leadership because they arrive late.

The other shortcoming of MRDs is that they are long and not thoroughly read. They contain so much detail that they obscure the key objectives of the project.

The product concept document is really a mini-requirements document, a brief vision statement. Some projects will still need a detailed requirements document; others may not, depending on the size of the engineering team and the complexity of the product.

48. The Written Business Plan (page 127)

The Successful Business Plan: Secrets and Strategies, by Rhonda M. Abrams is a good book on how to write a traditional business plan. It is particularly strong if you are seeking venture capital. It includes examples and anecdotes from executives and venture capitalists.

49. The Business Plan Outline (page 129)

Amateur financials are fine for your planning, but don't present them to financial pros. A poorly constructed financial plan can undermine a great business plan. Once you have a sponsor, have them recommend a pro to help with the financials. For internal planning, use the Small Business Administration's *Start-Up Costs Worksheet* reprinted in *Starting on a Shoestring: Building a Business Without a Bankroll* by Arnold S. Goldstein, or the more extensive worksheets in chapter 13 of *The Successful Business Plan: Secrets and Strategies* by Rhonda M. Abrams.

GLOSSARY

.com Abbreviation for commercial on the Internet. It identifies an Internet address of a business. Educational institutions use .edu. Government agencies use .gov and nonprofit agencies use .org.

401k A tax-deferred retirement plan. Rules vary from company to company, but in many companies, employees may borrow from their 401k retirement accounts. These loans can become problematic when you change companies or start your own business.

Back-of-a-Napkin As in "back-of-a-napkin design," which refers to engineers and executives designing products over lunch, sketching diagrams on whatever paper is at hand—often the back of an envelope or a napkin.

Bookmark A feature of Web browsers that returns the user to a specific Web page. This enables users to quickly revisit Web sites and check for updated information. Bookmarks are invaluable when doing market research. They enable the reader to first survey a topic and later revisit sites to gather more detailed information.

Brainstorm A group-planning technique that discourages evaluation and criticism during the early stages of problem solving. This technique yields innovative solutions, often with strong organizational support. (See pages 84 and 85.)

Breakthrough Pricing A price reduction strategy used to expand the overall size of a market. (See page 18.)

Channel Strategy Describes how to market, sell, and distribute a product. (See pages 78 and 79.)

Cost of Goods   Sometimes abbreviated COGS, this includes the cost of the material, labor, and overhead allocated to the manufacture of a product. (See page 45.)

Gross Margin   Net sales minus cost of goods.

Hard Drive   A storage device for a personal computer.

Hardware   A computer, part of a computer, or a collection of computers.

Intel   The world's largest manufacturer of microprocessors for personal computers.

Intuit   Developers of Quicken and TurboTax. (See page 8.)

IPO   Initial Public Offering or "going public." A company's stock is sold to the public for the first time. This is a major milestone for a Silicon Valley start-up and usually indicates some degree of revenue or success. Frederick D. Lipman in his book, *Going Public: Everything You Need to Know to Turn a Private Enterprise into a Publicly Traded Company,* steps the business owner through the details of going public. Chapter 14 chronicles Microsoft's IPO (reprinted from the July 21, 1986, issue of *Fortune* magazine).

Mantra   A word or phrase used repeatedly. Originally a mantra referred to words repeated as part of a Hindu meditation.

Memory   A key component of computers that stores instructions and data. Memory, unlike a hard drive, is usually directly accessible by the microprocessor and is usually based on semiconductor (silicon) technology.

Microprocessor   The brains of a personal computer and many other electronic devices including most:

- Calculators
- Stereo systems
- Video games

- Cellular phones
- Pagers
- Satellites
- Navigation systems
- Talking greeting cards

Microsoft   The world's leading developer of software for personal computers.

P&L   Profit and loss statement. The part of a company's financial statement that analyzes their profitability. Also called an Income Statement or an Operating Statement. Product or division-level P&Ls can help determine which products or divisions are profitable.

QA   Quality assurance. The QA department tests products under development to ensure that they work correctly. QA departments are often the unsung heroes of high-tech enterprises, meticulously testing and retesting products as engineering enhances them.

   Many companies also apply QA techniques to product names, new packaging, and advertising to ensure their effectiveness. This marketing QA function usually requires focus groups or customer interviews. (See also, page 59.)

R&D   Research and Development. R&D sounds like a single function, but in most companies, it designates two separate departments. The quality of communication and teamwork between the research and development departments often foreshadow the success of an enterprise. If R&D are geographically separate and continually bickering, research technology rarely appears in new products. If R&D are in the same building and report to one manager, the pace of innovation improves—often dramatically. Some start-ups may outperform their larger, more established competitors because they put

researchers and developers in the same office reporting
to one manager.

ROI   Return on investment. Analogous to the interest rate a
bank pays on a savings account, ROI measures the return
on a business investment.

Semiconductor   Usually made from silicon or germanium,
semiconductors have the unique property of conducting
electricity sometimes, but not always. They do not con-
duct electricity as well as most metals, thus the name
semiconductor. Semiconductor manufacturers exploit
this unique electrical property. Using ultraviolet light,
they print microscopic diagrams and pictures of circuits
on thin slices of semiconductor. Synonym: **chip.**

Memory chips are semiconductors that remember
data, instructions, pictures, and sound. Microprocessors
are semiconductors that do things. Following instructions, they add, compare, move, and route information.
Most consumer products with semiconductors have
both memory chips and microprocessors.

Silicon Valley   Named after the silicon used in microprocessor
and memory chips, Silicon Valley refers to the area surrounding Stanford University that is home to thousands
of high-tech companies. Northern Californians disagree
about the exact boundaries of Silicon Valley. Most observers would include the cities from Menlo Park to San
Jose, which encompasses Sunnyvale, Mountain View,
Palo Alto, and Cupertino.

The Valley   Short for Silicon Valley (see above).

VC   Short for Venture Capital or Venture Capitalist, as in, "Do
you have any VC funding?" Over fifty Silicon Valley VCs
reside in Menlo Park on Sand Hill Road surrounding Saint
Bede's Episcopal Church. The *San Jose Mercury News* sum-
marizes Silicon Valley VC activity several times each year.

Windows 95   A popular version of Microsoft's Windows operating system that was originally scheduled for release in 1995. Successor to Windows 3.1.

The Web   Short for World Wide Web or the Internet. The Web is a worldwide electronic cooperative with no real owner. It enables users to send, receive, and request information. There are three levels of participation in the Web. The first is sending and receiving e-mail. The second is visiting—or viewing—other peoples' and companies' Web sites. The third is to have your own personal or company Web site with information about you or your product.

Originally developed for the military, the Web refers to its spiderweb-like design that would continue to function even if many strands were cut during a nuclear war.

INDEX

ELTON B. SHERWIN, JR., grew up in the Bay Area, graduated from the University of California at Berkeley, and has spent his entire adult life in the high-tech arena, much of it in the Silicon Valley. Currently, Sherwin directs business planning and worldwide marketing for a leading Silicon Valley company. His products have won many awards, among them, *Byte* magazine's COMDEX Award for the Best New Technology. He lives in Menlo Park with his wife, Katharine, and their two daughters.